Jacqueline Kennedy Onassis

Legendary First Lady

Donna Brown Agins

Enslow Publishers, Inc.

40 Industrial Road   PO Box 38
Box 398   Aldershot
Berkeley Heights, NJ 07922   Hants GU12 6BP
USA   UK

http://www.enslow.com

With love and gratitude
to Richard, Spencer, and Garrett Agins

Library of Congress Cataloging-in-Publication Data

Agins, Donna Brown.
    Jacqueline Kennedy Onassis : legendary first lady / Donna Brown Agins.
      v. cm. — (People to know)
    Includes bibliographical references and index.
    Contents: Jackie dazzles Paris—Privileged beginnings—Adventure and romance—Political partner—Life as First Lady—Champion of the arts—Death in Dallas—Moving on—Calm waters—A life well lived.
    ISBN-10: 0-7660-2186-6 (hardcover)
    1. Onassis, Jacqueline Kennedy, 1929–1994—Juvenile literature. 2. Presidents' spouses—United States—Biography—Juvenile literature. 3. Celebrities—United States—Biography—Juvenile literature. [1. Onassis, Jacqueline Kennedy, 1929–1994 2. First ladies. 3. Women—Biography.] I. Title. II. Series.
CT275.O552A35 2004
973.922'092—dc22
   [B]   2003026956

ISBN-13: 978-0-7660-2186-0

Printed in the United States of America

10 9 8 7 6 5 4 3 2

Illustration Credits: AP/Wide World Photos, pp. 92, 108, 110; © Bettman/Corbis, p. 78; British Information Service/John Fitzgerald Kennedy Library, Boston, p. 88; Cecil Stoughton, White House/John Fitzgerald Kennedy Library, Boston, pp. 51, 73, 75, 80; David Berne/John Fitzgerald Kennedy Library, Boston, p. 14; Robert Knudsen, White House/John Fitzgerald Kennedy Library, Boston, pp. 6, 53, 65, 66, 84; Toni Frissell, Library of Congress, p. 35; U.S. Department of State/John Fitzgerald Kennedy Library, Boston, pp. 8, 9, 56; John Fitzgerald Kennedy Library, Boston, pp. 16, 20, 25, 29, 36, 97, 100, 102; U.S. Information Service/John Fitzgerald Kennedy Library, Boston, p. 62.

Cover Illustration: Photo courtesy of Robert Knudsen, White House/John Fitzgerald Kennedy Library, Boston.

Contents

Acknowledgments

Many thanks to James B. Hill, audiovisual archives specialist, John Fitzgerald Kennedy Library, Columbia Point, Boston, and to Sharon Ann Kelly, archives technician, John F. Kennedy Library and Museum. Both were knowledgeable guides to the resources available at the Kennedy Museum and Library.

Thanks, too, to my writing group, Edith, Judith, Karen, Jodie, Suzan, Marie, and Connie. For believing.

Jackie
Dazzles Paris

"Jackie! Jackie!" As the presidential motorcade drove through Paris on May 31, 1961, all eyes were fixed on one person. America's first lady, Jacqueline Bouvier Kennedy—known as Jackie—and her husband, John F. Kennedy, had come to France to meet with President Charles de Gaulle and his wife, Yvonne.

All along the boulevards, excited shouts of "Vive Jacqui!" filled the air. French and American flags fluttered from every lamppost. Presidents de Gaulle and Kennedy were powerful leaders of the Western world, but they were not the reason that half a million French citizens had come out that day. From the moment the Kennedys landed, the French press

Jacqueline Bouvier Kennedy Onassis

reported on all that Jackie did, said, and wore. America's first lady was an instant success.

Seven months earlier, in November 1960, Jackie's husband had been elected the thirty-fifth president of the United States. The youthful Kennedys were not well known around the globe. The U.S. State Department had warned the Kennedys not to expect a warm welcome in France. The French people tended to be reserved, and Charles de Gaulle was not easily impressed. President de Gaulle also had a distrust for anything that was not French.[1]

Since moving into the White House in January, the shy, quiet Jackie had doubted her ability as first lady. At forty-three, her husband was the youngest man ever elected president of the United States. Knowing this trip to Paris was important to her husband's success, Jackie had taped an interview, in advance, for a French television program.

The interview was filmed on the White House front lawn. Behind Jackie, workers scurried by with centerpieces, tables, and chairs, busily setting up for a dinner that night. Jackie ignored the flurry of activity as she answered the interviewer's questions in fluent French. When she could not think of a word in French, she said it in English with a French accent.

Jackie had lived in Paris for a year as a college student. She adored all things French and had even named her poodle, Gaullie, after General de Gaulle. She ended the interview by saying in perfect French, "I love France."[2] The program was aired in France before she arrived.

During Jackie Kennedy's three-day trip to Paris,

Mme. de Gaulle took her to see an infant-care nursing school. André Malraux, the minister of culture and a famous writer, escorted her to museums. Wherever Jackie went, huge crowds greeted her with cheers and applause. The French people adored Jackie's elegant sense of style, her poise, and her passion for the arts. But most of all, they admired her fluency in their language.[3] Her presence gave the French citizens a warmer feeling for America.

On the Kennedys last night in Paris, General and Madame de Gaulle hosted a grand six-course dinner in the Hall of Mirrors at the Palace of Versailles.

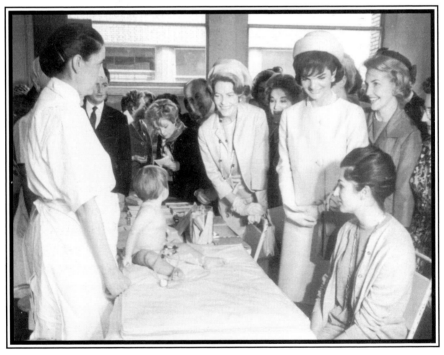

The first lady visited an infant-care nursing school in France.

"I now have more confidence in your country," said French president Charles de Gaulle after meeting Jackie.

Jackie usually wore clothing by American designers. But that evening, as a special gesture of diplomacy, she wore a glittering gown created by Givenchy, a native Parisian. Jackie's white satin dress honored the tricolored French flag with red and blue flowers embroidered on the bodice. Leaf-shaped diamond clusters sparkled in her hair.

Seated next to General de Gaulle, Jackie charmed him with her knowledge of the French arts and history. At one point, Jackie sent the translator away and personally interpreted the conversation between her husband and the French leader. De Gaulle was so impressed with Jackie and her knowledge of French history that he told President Kennedy, "I now have more confidence in your country."[4]

After the banquet, a ballet troupe performed for the guests. During the program, President de Gaulle and Jackie drew their chairs to the back of the box to talk privately without interpreters.

Later, on the way back to Paris, the presidential motorcade drove through the vast formal gardens of Versailles and then stopped at the main fountain on the grounds. The young couple stepped out of their car. Standing hand in hand, they watched cool sprays of water dance toward the night sky. After that evening, President Kennedy saw his wife in a new way. He recognized that she was a great political asset, and he appreciated her more than ever.[5]

Never before on a diplomatic trip had a first lady received more attention than the president. News of Jackie's success was broadcast in America. The visit to France was an early step in her transformation from a shy and unsure young woman into a confident first lady and worldwide celebrity. Speaking at a luncheon on June 2, 1961, President Kennedy told the audience of French businesspeople, "I am the man who accompanied Jacqueline Kennedy to Paris, and I have enjoyed it."[6]

Privileged Beginnings

On July 28, 1929, as the exciting, prosperous decade known as the Roaring Twenties was drawing to a close, Jacqueline Lee Bouvier was born into a family of wealth and privilege. Her father, John Vernou Bouvier III, nicknamed Jack, was an outgoing, handsome, thirty-eighty-year-old stockbroker. Her mother, the shy Janet Lee Bouvier, was a skilled horsewoman. She was sixteen years younger than her husband.

Jackie came home from the hospital to the Bouvier summer mansion in East Hampton, on New York's Long Island. The mansion was called Lasata, an American Indian word that means "place of peace."[1] From the time she was an infant, Jackie spent summers by the sea and winters in New York.

In those days, old Dutch windmills, ancient elm

trees, and small wooden cottages dating back to the 1600s made up the village of East Hampton. Lasata, one of the most lavish estates in the area, included several full-time gardeners, maids, a cook, and a chauffeur.

Over the years, both the Bouviers and the Lees had made millions of dollars from stock market and real estate investments. Although they had been neighbors on Park Avenue and in East Hampton, the two families were not friends. The Bouviers saw the Lee family as socially inferior.[2]

From the beginning, Jackie's parents' temperaments, goals, and views on life clashed. Her mother was a serious and practical person. Her father was fun-loving and reckless with money.

Jackie was three months old when the stock market crashed in October 1929. Overnight, the prosperous American economy was practically destroyed. High-priced stocks became worthless, and banks failed. Many people lost their jobs and life savings. Jack Bouvier lost most of his money. The family was forced to move to a smaller apartment on Park Avenue. Janet Bouvier's father, James Lee, owned the building and allowed his daughter and her family to live there rent-free.[3]

Both the Bouvier and the Lee families were Catholic. The relatives came together in New York at the church of St. Ignatius Loyola to celebrate Jackie's christening on December 22, 1929. She was given the name Jacqueline Lee. Her mother liked to pronounce it "Jack-leen." Her father insisted on calling her

"Jackie," the name friends and family used for the rest of her life.[4]

When Jackie turned three, she began learning about horses from her mother. Janet Bouvier kept a stable of four horses. A chestnut mare named Danseuse became Jackie's favorite.[5] Her mother gave her the mare as a gift.

On March 3, 1933, when Jackie was three and a half, her sister, Caroline Lee Bouvier, was born. The family called her Lee. From the beginning, the girls' personalities were different. Young Jackie was brave and outgoing; Lee was fearful and shy.

One day, their nanny took four-year-old Jackie and baby Lee to Central Park. Jackie wandered off. A police officer saw her and asked why she was alone. Jackie was not frightened or crying. She reported, "My nurse and baby sister seem to be lost."[6]

Jackie's love of books and reading began before she started kindergarten. By age five, she had read many books enjoyed by much older children. Often, when Jackie was supposed to be napping, she would climb out of bed, sit on the windowsill and read. Two of Jackie's heroes were Robin Hood and Mowgli from *The Jungle Book*.[7]

When it came time to start school in 1935, Jackie was enrolled in the Chapin School on East End Avenue in Manhattan. She studied reading, writing, arithmetic, and athletics, earning top grades. But she was also known as a troublemaker. Often Jackie finished her schoolwork before the other students. Bored, she would make noises and distract her classmates. Other times, she would sit in class and

Jackie was a bold child who loved to read and ride horses.

daydream. Boredom was just one of her school problems. She also hated wearing a uniform and rebelled against the strict discipline of the school.

A prankster who liked to play tricks on the teachers, Jackie was a ringleader among the girls. Once she even smeared face cream on the toilet seats at school.[8] When Jackie broke school rules, she was sent to Miss Stringfellow, the headmistress, who ordered her to behave. Jackie had her own interpretation of these occasions: One day, when her mother asked what happened in Miss Stringfellow's office, Jackie replied, "I go to her office, and Miss Stringfellow says, 'Jacqueline, sit down. I've heard things about you.' I sit down. Then Miss Stringfellow says a lot of things, but I don't listen."[9]

Meanwhile, the differences between Jackie's parents were leading to many bitter arguments. When Jackie turned seven, her parents separated. Even though the marriage had long been troubled, the family had appeared polite and calm to outsiders. This was a lesson Jackie took to heart: From an early age, she learned to keep her feelings to herself.

Jack Bouvier moved out of the family's Park Avenue apartment into a nearby hotel, and Jackie and Lee spent their weekends with their father. Every Saturday, he drove up to their apartment and honked his horn in a series of secret signals. The sisters raced out to the car, happy to spend time with him. Together, they enjoyed horse and buggy rides in Central Park, trips to the Bronx Zoo, and visits to the Metropolitan Museum of Art.

During the difficult times of her parents' marriage

and separation, riding and caring for her horse Danseuse provided an escape for Jackie. She enjoyed practicing and competing in horse shows. Jackie's entire family came to see her perform. The bigger the crowd, the better she rode.

Grandfather Bouvier, called Grampy Jack, was one of the most influential people of Jackie's childhood. From the time she was eight, Jackie spent Wednesday evenings after her dance class with Grampy Jack at his apartment on Park Avenue. They talked about everything from current events to the U.S. Constitution. He valued her opinion and treated her as an equal. Most valuable to Jackie was the time they spent reading and memorizing poetry. Grampy Jack wrote poems for Jackie and encouraged her to

Although she earned top grades at school, Jackie was known as quite a prankster by the teachers and her classmates.

write poetry that expressed her thoughts and feelings. She made up poems and stories about animals, often giving them human emotions. Jackie and Grampy Jack wrote letters back and forth, even though they lived near each other.

When Jackie was ten years old, her parents tried to mend their differences and make their marriage work for the sake of the children. The Bouviers rented a beach house for the summer. But instead of working out their problems, their relationship worsened. During this time, Jackie became shy and quiet.

In the small East Hampton community, there were no secrets. The neighbors all knew about the Bouviers' marital problems. In September 1939, Jackie's parents separated again. This time, the marriage ended. Janet Bouvier, Jackie, and Lee moved out of their Park Avenue apartment into a smaller apartment at One Gracie Square, near the Chapin School.

In those days, divorce was rare and not something people talked about openly. Also, divorce went against the rules of the Catholic Church. At family gatherings at Lasata, cousins made hurtful remarks about Jackie's parents' divorce. Jackie's classmates at school teased her, too. Jackie taught herself to shut out painful words she did not want to hear. Her sister, Lee, later said, "Jackie was really fortunate to have or acquire the ability to tune out, which she always kept."[10]

For Jackie, riding her horse gave her relief from family tensions. Soon she and Danseuse were clearing fences and racing at full speed. Jackie became an even more competitive horsewoman. At ten, she won a double victory in the junior horsemanship competition at the Madison Square Garden national championships.

Besides horses and books, Jackie loved the sea.[11] She enjoyed going to the beach to listen to the crashing surf and watch seagulls dive for fish. She composed poetry about the ocean, and in one of these poems, she wrote, "Oh to live by the sea is my only wish. . . ."[12]

A few days before Jackie turned eleven, her parents' divorce became final. But the anger between them did not stop with the divorce. For many years, they played tug-of-war for their daughters' affections. Jack Bouvier bought them expensive clothes and took Jackie and Lee on pony rides in the park and on trips to the New York Stock Exchange and matinees at Radio City Music Hall. Janet Bouvier, strict as always, set and enforced the family's rules. Their father easily won the contest for the girls' affections, and Jackie cherished the time she spent with him.[13]

Jack Bouvier shared with Jackie his ideas about what made a woman attractive. He believed in dressing well and having a personal style. Also, he told Jackie it was important to create an aura of privacy or mystery around herself—to hold something back, to act a little hard to get. He described to his daughter the ideal way to enter a room: eyes straight ahead, chin up, and smiling.

Though Jackie and Lee were close, they were often jealous of each other and competed for their father's attention. Jack Bouvier adored both of his daughters and was proud of them. But Jackie was his favorite. She, in turn, was devoted to him.[14]

Lee was considered the prettier of the two sisters. Jackie, known as the brainy one, resembled her father. She had the same wide-set eyes, dark coloring, high cheekbones, and broad smile. Jack Bouvier, also called "Black Jack" because of his deep year-round tan and slicked-back black hair, was movie-star handsome.

In June 1942, when Jackie was almost thirteen, Janet Bouvier married Hugh D. Auchincloss, an heir to the Standard Oil fortune. He owned two magnificent houses—Merrywood in McLean, Virginia, and Hammersmith Farm in Newport, Rhode Island. The marriage to "Uncle Hughdie" offered home and stability, two ingredients that had been missing from Jackie's life since her parents had separated and then divorced. Jackie and Lee also gained two stepbrothers, Yusha and Tommy, and a stepsister, Nina.

Despite this new stability in her life, Jackie's personality changed as she became a teenager. She had already learned to tune out when a situation made her uncomfortable. Now she spent many hours alone in her room reading, painting, and writing poetry. Even with her close girlfriends, Jackie was quiet and shy. She rarely spoke about anything personal. She kept her distance from boys.

In 1944, after she had been a student at Holton-Arms School in Bethesda, Maryland, for two years, Jackie was sent to an all-girls boarding school in Farmington, Connecticut. The school, called Miss Porter's, emphasized good manners and the art of

Jackie, top left, and her family: (1) Janet Auchincloss; (2) Hugh Auchincloss; (3) sister Lee; stepbrothers (4) Yusha and (5) Tommy; (6) stepsister Nina; and (7) baby Janet Jr.

conversation. Jackie earned an A-minus average, enjoyed her classes in art history and English literature, and became an editor of the school newspaper. She also drew a cartoon strip about a silly girl called "Frenzied Frieda," who got into all kinds of trouble.[15]

Although she was private and liked to read poetry, Jackie had a mischievous streak. She often broke school rules, sneaking late-night snacks from the school kitchen and once dumping a pie into an unpopular teacher's lap.

In 1945, while Jackie was away at Miss Porter's, her mother, Janet Auchincloss, gave birth to a baby girl, also named Janet. Sixteen-year-old Jackie wrote a poem about how delighted she was to have a new baby half-sister. Her half-brother, Jamie, was born in 1947.

At seventeen, Jackie graduated from Miss Porter's. Her entry in the yearbook stated that her ambition was "Not to be a housewife."[16] In a long-standing tradition, when young women from wealthy families turn eighteen they are formally introduced to society. This event is called a "debutante" party or "coming out" party. Jackie had her debutante party the summer after she graduated from Miss Porter's.

Although the coming out party meant little to her, Jackie fulfilled her role well, showing great poise and maturity as she greeted and charmed the guests. But books, education, and the arts—not parties—were her passions.

Soon, Jackie would be able to give those passions her full attention. She had been accepted to Vassar College and was about to begin a new life.

Adventure and Romance

Jackie entered Vassar College in Poughkeepsie, New York, in the fall of 1947. She enrolled in studio art classes to learn drawing and painting techniques. In her free time, she joined the dance group, worked on the college newspaper, and designed costumes for the drama club. Jackie was known on campus as having an offbeat sense of humor and being something of a loner. She chose literature as her major and made friends with other Vassar students whose main interests were books, writing, and the arts.

Always curious, Jackie loved learning. Her favorite class was the study of Shakespeare's writings.[1] She also especially liked her course on the history of religion. These were two of the most difficult courses that were offered at Vassar. Jackie earned an A-plus in both of them.

Shortly after arriving at Vassar, Jackie received an honor that embarrassed her more than it flattered her. A society columnist named Jackie "Debutante of the Year."[2] That was like being the queen of young high society. Jackie was featured in many newspaper articles, but she did not appreciate the attention. The publicity caused her to become even more guarded. She handled the situation by ignoring it and going on with her life.

Jackie's cousin John Davis later recalled asking how she felt about being named Debutante of the Year. "She was much prouder of making the Dean's List during her first term at Vassar," he said.[3] Jackie may not have been impressed with the honor, but many young men were. She had an active social life, though she did not have one special boyfriend.

In January of Jackie's freshman year, Grampy Jack died at the age of eighty-three. Grampy Jack had always encouraged his granddaughter's interests in history, literature, and poetry. He had been an important early influence on her, and Jackie had saved all of his letters. At the funeral, she slipped a bouquet of pansies into the coffin as a farewell to her grandfather. When she inherited $3,000 from Grampy Jack, she decided to use the money for a summer trip to Europe.

Jackie prepared for her travels as if she were studying for a final exam. She read about European history and pored over art books. She continued to study French. She even learned to speak some Italian and German.

In August 1948, soon after Jackie turned nineteen, she traveled with three girlfriends and a chaperone to England, France, Switzerland, and Germany. Jackie particularly enjoyed her time in Paris. The Palace of Versailles delighted her with its fancy gardens and elegant rooms. The group stayed at the dazzling palace until closing time because Jackie's girlfriends could not persuade her to leave. Jackie enjoyed France so much that she vowed to return. She wrote to her mother, "I've had a glimpse. Next time I want to soak it all up."[4]

Jackie returned to Vassar for her sophomore year. One day, she saw a notice on a bulletin board telling about the Smith College Junior Year Abroad program. Students from other schools could apply, too. With her excellent grades, Jackie was accepted into the program. But there was one condition: First she had to spend six weeks in an intensive language course at the University of Grenoble in the mountains of France.

That summer, just after her twentieth birthday, Jackie enrolled at the University of Grenoble. She spent the weekdays fine-tuning her French language skills. She wrote home to her mother, "I have an absolute mania now about learning to speak French perfectly."[5] On weekends, Jackie and her school friends visited villages in the countryside around Grenoble. Jackie explored small towns and waded in rivers. Once, when Jackie and her friends were eating

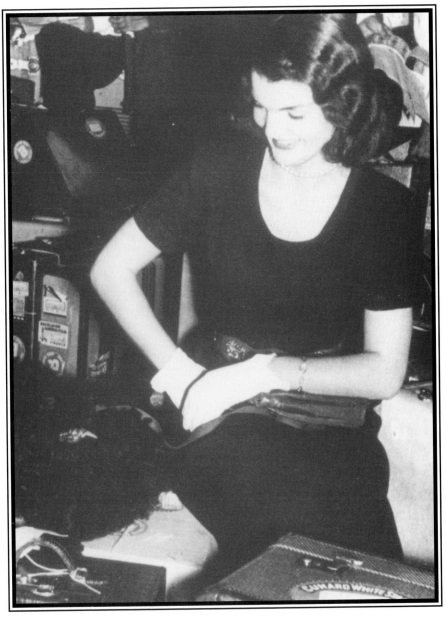

Jackie is all packed and ready for her trip to Europe.

a leisurely dinner, they missed the last tram back to the university. They had to walk five miles.[6]

In October, Jackie moved to Paris and enrolled in the Sorbonne University to study French literature and history. Jackie later said of her junior year abroad in France, "I loved it more than any year of my life. . . . I learned not to be ashamed of a real hunger for knowledge, something I had always tried to hide."[7]

Most American students lived in a dormitory while attending the Sorbonne. But Jackie and two friends wanted to live with a French family where only French was spoken. They rented a room in the apartment of Countess Guyot de Renty and her family.

Like many residences in Europe at that time, the countess's apartment had no central heat. Winters in Paris are cold. To stay warm while doing her home-work, Jackie wore sweaters, woolen stockings, and earmuffs.

All seven people living in the apartment shared one bathroom, with an old tin bathtub. Hot water was scarce. One icy day, Jackie wanted to take a hot bath. She turned up the temperature on the water heater. The water heater exploded and shattered the bath-room window.

When she had free time in Paris, Jackie walked along the banks of the Seine River, traveled on the Metro (subway), and ate at sidewalk cafés. She enjoyed Parisian art galleries and jazz clubs. "The most wonderful thing here is all the operas and theaters and ballets and how easy they are to get to" and how cheap, she said.[8] Jackie often visited the

Louvre art museum and enrolled in an art history class there.

When Jackie's school year in Paris ended, she stayed in France to see more of the country. This was a time of independence and discovery for her. With no special travel schedule, Jackie went where her heart led her. She visited châteaux (French mansions), small towns, gardens, and museums. For Jackie, it was the happiest and most carefree time she would ever know.[9]

After touring France, Jackie joined her stepbrother Yusha Auchincloss for a three-week trip to Ireland and Scotland. Jackie enjoyed stopping to talk to shopkeepers, farmers, or anyone who would speak with her. She was interested in people and the stories they told.[10]

Jackie decided not to return to Vassar College for her senior year. Instead, she enrolled at George Washington University in Washington, D.C. Jackie declared a major in French literature. She also took classes in creative writing and journalism. "I wanted to know people better. I thought studying journalism would be a great chance," she said.[11]

That fall, Jackie's mother saw an ad in *Vogue* magazine for the sixteenth annual Prix de Paris (Prize of Paris) writing contest for college seniors. The winner of the contest would spend six months in Paris and six months in *Vogue*'s New York City office. Jackie immediately entered the contest. She was one of 1,280 applicants from 225 colleges. Jackie won with an essay titled "People I Wish I Had Known."[12]

Hugh Auchincloss, Jackie's stepfather, worried

that if Jackie spent another year in Paris she would never want to come home. He convinced his wife that another year in Paris would not be good for her daughter. Disappointed, Jackie turned down the prize.[13] She explained, "I guess I was too scared to go to Paris again. I felt then that if I went back, I'd live there forever."[14] To make up for her disappointment, the Auchinclosses agreed to send Jackie and her sister, Lee, to Europe that summer.[15]

The Auchinclosses paid for the girls' trip, but they did not spoil them with expensive rooms. The sisters traveled third-class on the voyage across the ocean and were constantly getting caught trying to sneak into first-class areas of the ship.[16] Jackie and Lee enjoyed traveling to Spain, Italy, and England. When they returned home, the sisters wrote and illustrated a book, *One Special Summer*, about their trip.

That fall, twenty-two-year-old Jackie looked for her first paying job. Her stepfather arranged for her to have an interview at the *Washington Times-Herald* newspaper. Jackie told the editor she knew how to use a camera and persuaded him to hire her to write and photograph a column called "The Inquiring Camera Girl."[17] In truth she had no idea how to use a professional photographer's camera. After getting the job, Jackie secretly signed up for an intense course in news photography.

As the "Inquiring Camera Girl," Jackie stopped people on the street and asked them a funny, probing question. Then she took photos to publish alongside their answers. Once, Jackie asked several women, "Do you think a wife should let her husband think he is smarter than she is?"[18] Another time, outside a dental clinic, she asked, "Are men braver than women in the dentist's chair?"[19] Jackie, who rarely talked about herself, had the ability to get people to open up and offer their personal opinions.

One evening, at a party in Washington, Jackie met John Husted, a young stockbroker from New York. They immediately hit it off. After dating for a month, they became engaged. John and Jackie wrote letters when they were apart and visited each other on

For her first job after college, Jackie roamed the streets as the "Inquiring Camera Girl" for the Washington Times-Herald *newspaper. Then, in the office, she wrote articles for the paper.*

weekends. Eventually Jackie grew tired of traveling back and forth between Washington and New York. Besides, she enjoyed her work and independence. The romance began to cool.

Several months later, on a warm spring night in 1951, Jackie was invited to a dinner party given by Charles and Martha Bartlett. The Bartletts seated Jackie near a handsome Massachusetts congressman, John Fitzgerald Kennedy. Congressman Kennedy, age thirty-five, was a confirmed bachelor. Jackie and Jack, as he was known, talked to each other all evening.

Charles Bartlett and Congressman Kennedy walked Jackie to her car. The Bartletts' fox terrier, Josie, ran ahead of them. When Kennedy opened the door of Jackie's car, the dog barked and jumped inside. Wanting to surprise her, a man Jackie had been dating was sitting in the backseat. Congressman Kennedy left quickly. Jackie did not see him again for seven months.[20]

Jackie continued working for the *Times-Herald*, and Kennedy was preparing to run for the Senate. But he had not forgotten Jackie. He called her and they went dancing on their first date. Jackie knew that Jack Kennedy was older and enjoyed being single. Still, she was drawn to him. She decided that dating him would be worth the heartbreak even if things did not work out.[21] She called off her engagement to John Husted.

The young couple had many common interests. They both enjoyed studying history and poetry, were family oriented, took pleasure in travel, and loved the sea. Jack Kennedy appreciated Jackie's sense of humor, intelligence, and wide-ranging interests. The two soon began to see each other regularly, often going to dinner parties at the homes of friends. Sometimes they went to a movie with Jack's younger brother Bobby and his wife, Ethel.

On July 4, 1952, Jackie met the Kennedy family at their white-shingled house in Hyannis Port, on Cape Cod, Massachusetts. Jackie thought they were a welcoming, lively group. The family included Jackie in games of touch football, tennis, softball, and golf. She found the nonstop activity overwhelming.[22]

The Kennedys' love of competition even carried over to mealtimes. They often erupted into contests of who could speak the loudest or who knew the most about a subject. "How can I explain these people?" Jackie later asked. "They were like carbonated water, and other families might be flat."[23]

But after her first few visits, Jackie often found her time with the Kennedy family strained. Jackie, age twenty-three, had been athletic all her life, but she was neither competitive nor tough. Once, she even broke her ankle during a rough game of touch football. From that time on, she avoided the constant roughhouse activities. She stayed true to her own calm style, quietly maintaining her independence. She later said to a friend, "They'll kill me before I ever get to marry him. I swear they will."[24]

While the Kennedy brothers and sisters played sports or debated politics, Jackie sat on the porch talking with her future father-in-law, Joseph Kennedy. He was well informed and friendly. Jackie appreciated that his wife, Rose, was disciplined, a trait she shared with Jackie's mother.[25]

Joseph Kennedy, a former ambassador to England, could be bossy, stubborn, and arrogant. But Jackie was not afraid of him, and he respected that about her. Joe Kennedy shared his thoughts and often joked with Jackie. He wanted his son to be president. Joe Kennedy felt Jackie's grace, style, and intelligence would be a great help to his son politically.[26]

After winning a close election, Jack Kennedy took his seat in the U.S. Senate in 1952. That same year, General Dwight D. Eisenhower became the nation's thirty-fourth president. Senator Kennedy escorted Jackie to Eisenhower's presidential inaugural ball. By then, their dating had turned into a courtship.

In May 1953, Jackie traveled to England with a friend to cover the June 2 coronation of Queen Elizabeth II for the *Times-Herald*. Just before she left for London, Jack Kennedy proposed marriage to Jackie. She left without giving him an answer.

Political Partner

Jackie's stories about Queen Elizabeth's coronation in London were a great success. Her articles for the *Times-Herald* often appeared on the newspaper's front page in Washington, D.C.

When Jackie found herself with free time in London, she browsed in bookstores. After the coronation, Jackie and her friend went to Paris for a week's vacation. Jackie toured Paris and went to even more bookstores. Sometime during that week, Jackie confided in her friend that she was in love with Jack Kennedy. But she also felt frightened that her life would be taken over by politics if she married him. Her friend later said that Jackie "always wanted to be herself, and I think that losing her own personality was what she was most worried about."[1]

At the airport before leaving for home, Jackie paid more than $100 in excess fare for her heavy luggage. Her suitcases were filled with books—presents for Senator Kennedy.

When she returned from England, Jackie accepted Jack Kennedy's marriage proposal. She told a friend that she felt like the luckiest girl in the world. The future Mrs. Kennedy wanted a small private wedding. But Joseph Kennedy, insisting that his son was a public figure, demanded that the couple have a large wedding with plenty of newspaper publicity.

Jackie wanted her fiancé to meet her father. Jack Bouvier and Jack Kennedy met in a New York restaurant. The two men enjoyed each other's company, and this was the start of a long, close friendship. Jackie's father had some advice for his future son-in-law: "If you ever have trouble with Jackie, just put her on a horse."[2] Jack Bouvier approved of Jackie's plans to marry Kennedy and agreed to escort his daughter down the aisle on her wedding day.

Bouvier arrived in Newport, Rhode Island, several days before the September wedding, expecting to be included in the prenuptial parties. But Jackie's mother did not invite her ex-husband to any of the festivities. The divorced couple still had hard feelings. On the morning of the wedding, two cousins were helping Jack Bouvier dress for the ceremony. It soon became clear that he had been drinking, though he insisted that he felt well enough to walk Jackie down the aisle. The cousins phoned Jackie's mother.

Worried that her ex-husband would embarrass himself and the family, Jackie's mother decided that

Jackie's stepfather would walk the bride down the aisle instead. Jackie dearly loved her father and wanted him to be her escort, but her mother was firm.[3]

On the Kennedy's sunny but windy wedding day, September 12, 1953, thousands of well-wishers gathered outside St. Mary's Church in Newport. Jackie entered the church on the verge of tears.[4] Within a

The future looked bright for Jacqueline Lee Bouvier and John Fitzgerald Kennedy on their wedding day.

few moments, she managed to rise above her disappointment.

Jackie never showed her emotions publicly. No matter what she thought or felt, she always behaved graciously. Hugh Auchincloss walked his smiling stepdaughter down the aisle. There, in front of six hundred guests, twenty-four-year-old Jacqueline Lee Bouvier married thirty-six-year-old John Fitzgerald Kennedy. Twelve hundred people came to the wedding reception at Hammersmith Farm. The newlyweds left for their honeymoon in Acapulco, Mexico, after cutting the cake.

Jackie wrote her father a letter of compassion and

The newlyweds honeymooned in Acapulco.

forgiveness as soon as she arrived in Acapulco. She told him that in her heart, he was the one who had walked her down the aisle.[5]

The Kennedys had no home of their own the first winter of their marriage. They split their time between the Auchincloss home, Merrywood, in Virginia, and the Kennedy family home in Hyannis Port.

Jackie had not been interested in politics before she married Senator Kennedy. Now she learned as much as she could about the subject. She went back to school to study American History at the Georgetown School of Foreign Service. She went to the opening sessions of Congress and listened to committee hearings on which Senator Kennedy served. She often drove her husband to his office and stayed to help.

Jackie had a direct effect on many things in Jack Kennedy's life. She listened to him practice his speeches, encouraging him to lower his voice and speak slowly for dramatic effect.[6] Senator Kennedy's speeches often contained quotes that Jackie had translated from French literature.[7] When her husband could not attend a function, she went instead. Along with Jackie's new political responsibilities came more press coverage. Although Jackie was never comfortable with publicity, reporters were impressed with her poise and intelligence.[8]

Jackie also helped her husband by her ability to judge a person's character. She told him who was trustworthy and who was a phony. Senator Kennedy valued and relied on his wife's judgment. They were political partners in public, but the senator and his wife were always totally private about personal matters.

Back in his college days, Senator Kennedy had suffered a sports-related back injury. Several years later, while serving in the navy during World War II, he injured his spine when his boat, *PT109*, sank. In 1954, during their first year of marriage, his back problems returned.

Jackie accompanied her husband to New York for spinal surgery, a dangerous and serious operation. The surgery was a failure and, worse, a bad infection set in. Jackie never left her husband's bedside. At midnight on October 21, 1954, doctors told the family that Senator Kennedy was near death. A Catholic priest was called in to administer the last rites, given when there is no hope of recovery. Jackie never wept or became angry. Instead, she read her husband poetry, told him jokes, and helped the nurses take care of him.

Senator Kennedy did not die. In fact, six weeks later he was well enough for the operation to be repeated. This time the surgery was successful. The young couple moved into the Kennedy family home in Palm Beach, Florida, for Jack Kennedy's recovery. Over the next seven months, Jackie cleaned his surgical wound and changed his bandages.

To keep his spirits up, she read to him and joked around to make him laugh. When her husband was well enough to work, Jackie helped with his Senate tasks by relaying information from Senator Kennedy to his secretary.

One afternoon, Jackie was taking notes while her

husband spoke about courageous political leaders. She urged him to write a book about the leaders he admired. Jackie helped with the research, wrote while he dictated, and edited his writing. Senator Kennedy's book *Profiles in Courage* won a Pulitzer Prize, an award given annually for excellence in literature. On one of the opening pages, he wrote that he could never "adequately acknowledge the help his wife provided . . . the book would not have been possible without her."[9]

By August 1955, Senator Kennedy felt strong enough to travel to Europe as a member of the Senate Foreign Relations Committee. The Kennedys visited Poland. They had an audience with the Pope in Italy. In France, Jackie acted as translator between her husband and former French Premier Georges Bidault. Of Jackie, Bidault said, "Never have I encountered so much wisdom invested with so much charm."[10]

That year, Jackie was happy to learn that she was pregnant. The couple purchased a large house, Hickory Hill, in McLean, Virginia, not far from Merrywood, where Jackie's mother lived. Jackie began to remodel and decorate their new home. Sadly, a few months later, her pregnancy ended in a miscarriage.

Early in 1956, Jackie found out she was pregnant again. She created a cheerful nursery and spent her time sprucing up Hickory Hill. At that time, the Democratic Party was considering naming Senator Kennedy its vice-presidential nominee. Though Jackie was eight months pregnant, she traveled in July to the Democratic convention, where the candidate would be named. Both Jackie and her husband were disappointed when he did not receive the nomination.

In August, still tired from the stress of the convention, Jackie felt sudden, painful stomach cramps. Her husband was in Europe, so Jackie's mother drove her to the hospital. Doctors performed emergency surgery to deliver the baby, but it was too late. Senator Kennedy's brother Bobby told Jackie the sad news and took care of the burial arrangements. Jackie named the baby girl Arabella.[11] A few days later, Senator Kennedy arrived home from Europe to be with his grieving wife.

The Kennedys sold Hickory Hill to Bobby and his wife, Ethel, who already had a growing family. The Kennedys then rented a home in Georgetown, a neighborhood of Washington, D.C. This was a difficult period in their marriage. They found it hard to talk about their grief over losing the baby. Also, there was a big difference in their ages, and they no longer shared many of the same interests. Jackie was interested in culture and the arts. Her husband's main concern now was his ambition to be president. Soon the emotional distance between them became a physical distance as well.[12]

Senator Kennedy spent many days traveling for political reasons, leaving his wife alone. When he was away from home on weekends, Jackie went to Merrywood to ride horses in the countryside. The following year, she became pregnant again.

In July 1957, her father, Jack Bouvier, fell ill. Jackie was five months pregnant. She planned to visit him in New York the following week. But on August 1,

Jackie's father went into a coma. Jackie and her husband quickly made travel arrangements, but her father died before they arrived. His nurse said that the last word he spoke was "Jackie."[13]

Several years earlier, Jackie's sister, Lee, had married Prince Stanislas Radziwill and moved to London. So Jackie alone made all of her father's funeral arrangements. At the funeral mass, she arranged for white baskets filled with white summer flowers, to be placed near her father's coffin. She described them as looking "like Lasata in August."[14] Before the casket was closed, Jackie slipped a bracelet into her father's hand. It was the gift he had given to her when she graduated from Miss Porter's school.

A few months later, on the day after Thanksgiving, 1957, Jackie gave birth to a healthy daughter, Caroline Bouvier Kennedy. The Kennedys moved into a new home in Georgetown when Caroline was three weeks old. Motherhood brought a sense of peace and great happiness to Jackie.[15]

When Senator Kennedy ran for reelection to the Senate in 1958, Jackie proved to be an excellent campaigner. She traveled with her husband and met voters throughout Massachusetts. The crowds were twice as large when Jackie appeared with him.

Senator Kennedy was elected to his second term on November 4, 1958. Over the next two years, he spent most of his time traveling around the United States giving speeches and making his name known to voters. Senator Kennedy had unofficially begun his campaign for the Democratic nomination for the presidency.

The summer of 1960 was a bright time for Jackie. She was pregnant again, and Senator Kennedy won the Democratic Party's nomination for president. Lyndon Baines Johnson, a senator from Texas, was chosen as his vice-presidential running mate. The morning after the Democratic convention, Jackie held her first press conference as a potential first lady.

Although Jackie was pleased that her husband had won the presidential nomination, he had several definite obstacles to overcome in order to win the election. Many people considered him too young and inexperienced to be president. Also, JFK, as he was known, did not define himself as a liberal or a conservative. He described himself as a realist. Many Democrats feared that people in the extreme wings of the party would not support him.

For Kennedy, the major obstacle was his religion. In the history of the United States, only one other Catholic had run as a major-party candidate for president. That was in 1928, when Democrat Alfred E. Smith was badly defeated by Herbert Hoover. During his campaign, JFK assured people that if he were elected president, he would support the Constitution and uphold the separation of church and state.

Jackie knew it would be a tough race, and she wanted to campaign with her husband. Her doctor, fearing a repeat of earlier miscarriages, advised her to stay home. Jackie was torn between the desire to help her husband win the presidency and her fear of losing the baby. She came up with an answer for her predicament.

From their home in Georgetown, Jackie worked to

help her husband get elected. Placing a conference call to eleven women in eleven states, she enlisted women in a nationwide campaign, Calling for Kennedy. She also helped organize the Women's Committee for New Frontiers, a group that met several times to discuss health care for the elderly, unemployment, and education issues. Jackie wrote a weekly column called "Campaign Wife," which was published in several newspapers. She composed thousands of letters to voters and talked with women leaders about questions of importance to them. Jackie gave press conferences in Hyannis Port and Washington, D.C. Even as the due date for her baby's birth grew closer, Jackie appeared on television shows to support her husband.

Journalists from newspapers and magazines often came to Georgetown to interview her. The reporters and photographers usually wanted pictures of the Kennedys' family life. Jackie cooperated, but she was uneasy with the invasion of her privacy.

Eventually Jackie came to appreciate politics, saying, "It's the most exciting life imaginable—always involved with the news of the moment."[16] Kenny O'Donnell, one of her husband's close aides, said that Jackie, "was always cheerful and obliging, never complaining." He found her "refreshing" because she did not "put on a show of phony enthusiasm about everything" on the campaign trail.[17]

Near the end of the campaign, Jackie rejoined her husband on the road, saying, "If he lost, I'd never forgive myself for not being there."[18] In various parts of the country, Jackie gave speeches in different languages, winning Senator Kennedy some much-needed votes. In Puerto Rico, Jackie spoke Spanish; in the north end of Boston, she spoke Italian; at a Cajun Festival in New Orleans, she charmed her listeners with French.[19]

Jackie actively sought out the African-American vote, attending women's fundraising dinners and visiting African-American churches.[20] Of all the places she traveled to, Jackie was most troubled by the poverty in West Virginia. She told of "little children on rotting porches, with pregnant mothers . . . young mothers all their teeth gone from bad diet." They were images she never forgot.[21]

The final test of the campaign was the first televised presidential debate. At that time, television was a relatively new medium. Jackie invited different women's groups to watch the debate with her at home. Onscreen, John F. Kennedy looked strong, intelligent, and alert. His opponent, Republican vice president Richard M. Nixon, appeared tired and sweated profusely. Seventy million Americans watched the debate. JFK's popularity surged. Still, there was the issue of JFK's religion: Would Americans elect a Catholic president?

Jackie described the night of the extremely close election as "the longest night in history."[22] The next morning, after she learned that her husband had been elected president, Jackie went out for a walk. She knew her own life would be forever changed. At thirty-one, Jackie was about to become America's first lady.

Life as First Lady

As the third-youngest first lady in American history, Jacqueline Bouvier Kennedy knew she had been given a chance to make a great contribution to her country. She wanted to live up to the honor.[1] Although she was eight months pregnant when her husband won the presidential election, Jackie immediately began selecting members of her staff and organizing her family's move to the White House.

The Kennedys spent a quiet Thanksgiving at their home in Georgetown. The next day, November 25, 1960, Jackie was rushed to the hospital for emergency surgery to deliver her baby. She gave birth to a premature baby boy. Even though he was healthy,

John Fitzgerald Kennedy Jr. spent his first few days in an incubator.

Jackie used her recovery time in the hospital to plan her inaugural wardrobe. During the campaign, she had been criticized for her expensive tastes and her preference for French clothing. To avoid more disapproval, Jackie chose American designer Oleg Cassini to create her White House wardrobe.

Soon after Jackie's release from the hospital, John Jr. was baptized in a small Georgetown church. Following the ceremony, still weak from surgery, Jackie went directly to the White House to meet with the outgoing first lady, Mamie Eisenhower, the wife of Dwight D. Eisenhower. This meeting about overseeing the housekeeping of the White House was a tradition that had been followed by many first ladies.[2]

Jackie had first visited the public rooms of the White House when she was eleven years old. At that time, she had no idea that twenty years later she would call the executive mansion her home. Now, as Jackie visited the private family quarters, she saw a collection of shabby rooms with dirty carpets and peeling plaster. The public rooms contained a jumble of mismatched furniture. Jackie told her newly appointed press secretary that the mansion looked like "a hotel that had been decorated by a wholesale furniture store during a January clearance [sale]."[3]

The incoming first lady had a deep respect for history. She decided that restoring the mansion would be her contribution as first lady. To get started, she asked the mansion's chief usher, J. B. West, to show her the photographs and architectural studies of the White House.[4]

The Kennedys spent the next six weeks in Palm Beach, Florida, planning their move to the White House. Instead of resting and recovering from her surgery, Jackie studied blueprints and the history of the White House. Before the Kennedys moved in, Jackie knew exactly how she would go about restoring this historic treasure.[5]

A series of parties, called preinaugural galas, were scheduled for the night before JFK's inauguration. For these parties, designer Oleg Cassini had created a white satin gown and matching cape for Jackie. As with most of her clothing, the gown was simple but elegant. On the evening of the galas, people gathered in the streets to catch a glimpse of the incoming president and his wife as they rode by in their car. When he saw the crowds, president-elect Kennedy told an aide, "Turn on the lights so they can see Jackie."[6] Jackie attended only one of the many galas that night, and then she went home to rest.

In photos from that time, Jackie is always smiling. She looks healthy and energetic. But in reality, she was worn out from campaigning and weak from her surgery. She later said, "I was in physical and nervous exhaustion. . . . I always wished I could have participated more in those first shining hours with him, but at least I thought I had given him the son he longed for."[7]

By this time, Jackie had perfected her way of handling difficult or unpleasant situations. She never backed away from responsibility. She hid any negative feelings and behaved with grace and dignity.

The following day, January 20, 1961, the dazzling blue skies and gleaming white snow gave Washington, D.C., a magical feeling. The famous poet Robert Frost recited his poem "The Gift Outright" before John F. Kennedy took his presidential oath. Jackie had listened to bits and pieces of her husband's inaugural address for several weeks. But that morning was the first time she heard the entire speech, which outlined his plans for a new America.

In his speech, JFK challenged Americans to live their lives and solve their problems with imagination, innovation, and invention. He called this "The New Frontier." His most famous quote is from this inaugural address: "Let the word go forth from this time and place, to friend and foe alike, that the torch has been passed to a new generation of Americans. . . . And so, my fellow Americans: ask not what your country can do for you—ask what you can do for your country."[8]

After the ceremony, Jackie, who never displayed affection in public, touched her husband's cheek and said, "Jack, you were so wonderful."[9]

The first impact the new first lady had on America was in the area of fashion. Jackie wore a fawn-colored wool coat with a sable fur collar and matching dress to the inauguration. A pillbox hat—a domed brimless hat worn on the back of her head—completed Jackie's outfit. Her clothing set her apart from the other women in the crowd, who were dressed in dark-colored clothing and furs. Jackie looked young, fresh, and original.

Immediately, women all over the country wanted to look like Jackie. Within weeks, stores began selling copies of her clothing. The morning of the inauguration, Jackie had grabbed her hat to keep it from blowing away in a strong gust of wind. This put a small dent in the crown. Soon, women all over the country were ordering pillbox hats and putting a dent in them. Jackie made simple sleeveless dresses, low-heeled shoes, and pillbox hats popular. This was called the "Jackie look," and women of all ages tried to copy it.[10]

Jackie's style was not just about clothing, but also about a way of life that appreciated beauty, history, and classically elegant design. The impact of Jackie's style was soon felt in the executive mansion. The day after the inauguration, painters, plumbers, and carpenters began work on the private quarters of the White House.

Even though the renovation would make living there difficult, President and Mrs. Kennedy moved into the White House. Caroline and John Jr. stayed in Palm Beach at the home of their Kennedy grand-parents until their rooms were ready.

The Kennedys were the first family with young children to live in the White House since Theodore Roosevelt's administration in the early 1900s. The first lady took her new role seriously, but family time was her top priority. "I just wanted to save some normal life for Jack and the children and for me. My first fight was to fight for a sane life for my babies and their father."[11] To escape from the constant glare of the press, the Kennedys rented Glen Ora, a weekend home in Virginia. There, away from the White House, they cherished their privacy.[12]

In a very short time, Jackie transformed the upstairs private rooms of the White House into a warm, comfortable home. Once her family was settled in the new quarters, she turned her attention to the restoration of the public rooms of the executive mansion. But Jackie had used up her entire White House redecoration budget on the private rooms. "I know we are out of money, Mr. West," she told the head usher, "but never mind! We're going to find some way to get real antiques into this house."[13]

The first lady was issued more money by Congress. This was the last taxpayer money that was to be used for the restoration of the White House. Jackie then began a campaign to raise private donations for the rest of the project. She approached Henry Francis du Pont, curator of the Winterthur Museum in Wilmington, Delaware, and an authority on American decorative art.[14] He agreed to help. Then Jackie appointed Lorraine Pearce to be the first curator of the White House. Stéphane Boudin, a famous French decorator, also worked with Jackie on the restoration.

In the spring of 1961, three months after the Kennedys moved into the White House, two major world events made President Kennedy a target of criticism. First, the Soviet Union became the first nation to send a man into space. Second, Fidel Castro, the dictator of Cuba, stopped a United

For Jackie, family was always her number-one priority.

States–sponsored attempt to remove him from power. The invasion of Cuba became known as the Bay of Pigs, named for the place where the United States ships landed. Both events were seen as major setbacks for President Kennedy's administration. Critics pointed to his youth and inexperience as weaknesses in his presidency.

Jackie was concerned about the pressures of her husband's demanding job. She supported him, but also felt she should remain focused on her children and the restoration of the White House. She formed the White House Fine Arts Committee and the White House Restoration Committee to locate furniture, paintings, and antiques original to the White House or its time period.

When Jackie and Mr. West began hunting for historic items, they looked in closets, unused rooms, and storage spaces. Friends called these search trips "spelunking."[15] The word spelunking means to explore or study caves. But instead of caves, Jackie and Mr. West were exploring the White House attic, warehouses, and basement. Jackie's goal was to find objects from past presidents and display as many as possible throughout the White House.[16]

Jackie hunted for antiques in dusty storerooms and closets, sometimes on her hands and knees. One day, when she and Mr. West were rummaging through a closet, they found four one-hundred-year-old marble busts of presidents George Washington and Martin Van Buren and explorers Christopher Columbus and Amerigo Vespucci. Jackie hauled them out and had their cracked noses and ears repaired.

"*It was a new mystery story every day,*" *said Jackie in her hunt through the White House for antiques and other memorabilia from past presidents.*

She placed the busts on pedestals throughout the public rooms.[17]

On other spelunking trips, they discovered china that had been purchased by President Lincoln. In the cellar, they found woven rugs ordered by Theodore Roosevelt in 1902 for the Red Room and the Green Room. After sorting through 26,500 items in and around the executive mansion, Jackie said, "I had a backache every day for three months, but it was a new mystery story every day."[18]

At the same time Jackie was working on the White House restoration, she began preparing for her first overseas diplomatic trip. The first couple was scheduled to visit Canada, France, and Vienna, Austria. President Kennedy was in the world spotlight for another reason, too. On May 5, 1961, the United States launched a rocket into space. Alan Shepard Jr.'s 117-mile flight lasted only fifteen minutes, but he made history as the first American astronaut in space.

Meanwhile, the young first lady was an instant success in Canada. Jackie wowed the crowds when she wore a suit in the same color red as the uniforms of the Royal Canadian Mounted Police. She was cultured, stylish, and smart. To the world, the president's wife represented the youthful promise of her husband's administration.

In the early 1960s, the United States and the Soviet Union had great political differences. The two countries were also fiercely competitive in the race into outer space. The Soviets had sent the first human being into space when astronaut Yuri Gagarin orbited the earth on April 12, 1961. It was only weeks later that the United States had caught up, with Alan Shepard Jr.'s flight. Jackie was warned that a meeting with Soviet leader Nikita Khrushchev, scheduled for Vienna, would be tense. She understood that it would be a real test of her diplomatic skills.

President Kennedy and Premier Khrushchev met on June 3, 1961, speaking through translators. President Kennedy later admitted the talks had not gone well.[19] Jackie was more successful. When Khrushchev bragged that the Soviet Union had a better education system than the United States, Jackie answered with a playful, "Oh, Mr. Chairman, don't bore me with statistics."[20] Khrushchev was charmed and amused.

Still trying to prove Russia's superiority to the United States, Khrushchev boasted to Jackie about the Soviet lead in the space race. She ignored his comment and politely asked about the dog Strelka, which had been sent into orbit. This led to a friendly conversation about animals. Before she left Vienna, Khrushchev offered one of Strelka's puppies to Jackie. Several months later, the pup arrived at the White House. The Kennedys named it Pushinka, which is Russian for "Fluffy."[21]

After their European tour, President Kennedy went back to Washington. Jackie traveled to Greece with her sister for a week's vacation. Jackie and Lee toured the Parthenon and the Greek islands and had dinner with the Greek royal family. The first lady enjoyed herself so much that she said someday she would like to have a vacation home in Greece.[22]

The first lady shares a laugh with Nikita Khrushchev. Jackie charmed the usually gruff Soviet leader.

Back in Washington, D.C., Jackie wanted to safe-guard the antiques used in the restoration of the White House. Public Law 87-286 made the White House a national monument.

Jackie also knew that the restoration project would need ongoing funding. Her solution was to publish *The White House: An Historic Guide*. The millions of dollars earned from the guidebook's sales went directly to the White House Historical Association's purchasing fund. The complete restoration project cost more than $2 million.[23]

As their first year in the White House drew to a close, the first family spent the Christmas holiday in Palm Beach. Jackie was out swimming with Caroline and John when she learned that her father-in-law, Joseph Kennedy, had suffered a massive stroke. The stroke left him speechless and paralyzed on his left side. Jackie had enjoyed a special relationship with her father-in-law. Now, visiting him in the hospital, she kissed his distorted face and his disabled hand.[24]

President Kennedy had always turned to his father for advice and support. He now turned to Jackie for wisdom and comfort. In the most difficult times, both in public and private, Jackie always showed maturity beyond her years.[25]

Champion of the Arts

6

On Valentine's Day in 1962, millions of Americans tuned in to a television special, *A Tour of the White House with Mrs. John F. Kennedy*. Once again, Jackie chose a simple wool dress for the nationally televised tour. And once again, millions of women were impressed by Jackie's style and tried to imitate her.

Today, Kennedy's presidency is considered the first television administration. JFK had effectively used the new medium of television during the presidential election, and he continued to find it a useful way to communicate with the American public. As a result of the 1962 White House broadcast, Jackie won a special Emmy Award for public service, and cash donations flowed into the White House restoration fund.

As Jackie restored a sense of history to the White

House, she also modernized the style of presidential entertaining. Guests at the executive mansion enjoyed evenings that were more fun, casual, and cultured than in past administrations.[1]

Fireplaces crackled on cold nights, and ceiling lights were dimmed to the level of soft, glowing candlelight. Centerpieces created from flowers grown in government-owned greenhouses decorated round tables for six or eight. The young first lady broke with the old tradition of formal assigned seating by having guests draw their seating from slips of paper in a silver bowl. Everyone agreed that her parties were spectacular and well planned.[2]

Jackie felt that American arts should be represented at the White House. She believed that artists were central figures to the health of a country.[3] Jackie viewed culture as something of great importance to be passed down to future generations. To her, the word *culture* meant recognizing the best of the arts, religion, and customs that civilization has to offer.[4]

Jackie had a temporary stage built in the East Room, and the beautifully restored White House became a backdrop for evenings devoted to the arts. One night, the famed choreographer Jerome Robbins staged a ballet performance at the White House. Another evening, actors from the American Shakespeare Festival recited sonnets and passages from plays. Some nights, opera singers performed, while other evenings featured string quartets. Painters, poets, writers, musicians, and dancers were all represented during cultural evenings at the White House.[5]

Artists from around the world were grateful to

Jackie for her devotion to the arts. In the past, because of political differences, the famed Spanish cellist Pablo Casals had refused to play in the United States. But because of his high regard for Jackie, he played at the White House.[6] After the evening's concert, the first lady walked Mr. and Mrs. Casals to the door. It was a cold evening, and Jackie was not wearing a coat over her evening dress. The Casals were concerned that she would catch cold and had urged her to not come outside. But the first lady said, "The president would want me to—and I myself want to."[7] Jackie did not go inside until the Casals had driven away.

Because the first lady treasured culture, she wished to improve the status of the arts in the United States in other ways as well. Creating a government department of the arts became her long-range goal. In private, Jackie persuaded her husband to create the position of White House arts consultant. The first lady did not want it publicly known, but she had a great influence on her husband in this area, helping him gain a deeper appreciation of the role of the arts in society.[8]

Though only thirty-two, the first lady was in a position to influence American attitudes and policies. Before her husband's election, money had not been allocated to museums on a regular basis. Television, still quite new, had not been tapped as means of bringing education into American homes. Quietly, without fanfare, Jackie worked to encourage government funding for both of those areas. Despite her shyness, she made 175 public appearances, all of them having to do with the arts. She rarely spoke at the events she attended, but her presence gave the concert, play, or gallery opening importance and focused attention on the event.[9]

Jackie was eager to see Washington, D.C., become a cultural center like Paris and London. For years, people had dreamed of a large performing arts center in the nation's capital. In 1958, President Eisenhower had signed the legislation for a national arts center but budgeted only enough money to purchase the land.[10]

President Kennedy strongly supported the idea, and he asked Jackie and former first lady Mamie Eisenhower to help raise money to build the center. As one fundraiser, Jackie painted two designs for Christmas cards, which were sold to the public. It was a start, but millions of dollars would be needed before the dream of a national cultural center could become a reality.

Jackie had always enjoyed travel and seeing exotic parts of the world. In March 1962, she took her first official trip without her husband. Her sister, Lee Radziwill, accompanied Jackie on a goodwill tour of India and Pakistan. Their first stop was Italy. Pope John XXIII granted Jackie a thirty-two-minute private audience in his library at the Vatican. The first lady spoke with the Pope in French and gave him a signed copy of her husband's speeches. The Pope gave her a rosary and papal medals for Caroline and John Jr.[11]

When Jackie arrived in India, one hundred thousand people lined the streets on the road to

Jackie, center, and her sister, Lee, left, visited India to promote goodwill between India and the United States. Here, Jackie stands between Prime Minister Jawaharlal Nehru and his daughter, Indira Gandhi. At right, next to Nehru, is John Kenneth Galbraith, U.S. ambassador to India.

New Delhi. Villagers and farmers, with their ox-drawn carts parked wheel to wheel, chanted "*Ameriki Rani,*" which means American queen.[12] Prime Minister Jawaharlal Nehru, his daughter Indira Gandhi, and the U.S. Ambassador welcomed the first lady to their country.

Jackie's respect for their culture endeared her to the people of India. Throughout her trip, she wore clothing of the same colors used in Indian miniature paintings. Although she did not speak any of the Indian dialects, she participated in other aspects of the culture. Jackie had a traditional *tilak*, or red dot, painted on her forehead, wore a sari, rode an elephant, and put roses on the gravesite of the great Indian leader Mahatma Gandhi. When Jackie threw colored chalk to celebrate the holiday of *Holi*, her Secret Servicemen grumbled because the chalk powder was made from manure.[13]

One afternoon, Jackie joined Prime Minister Nehru in his garden. Together they watched a snake charmer play his pipe while a cobra swayed to the movement and music. Suddenly, a mongoose appeared. All at once, the show turned into a bloody fight between the snake and the mongoose. Jackie was frightened and backed into the prime minister in shock. It was one of the few times she ever became flustered in public.[14]

Jackie and Lee traveled by train to Benares, one of the oldest cities in the world. There, the sisters boarded a boat decorated with hundreds of yellow, red, and orange marigolds. The flowered barge carried Jackie and Lee past bathing spots and cremation platforms along the Ganges River. All along the banks of the waterway, crowds gathered to see Jackie. Some made loud, shrill sounds by blowing on conch shells. Other excited onlookers banged on metal triangles as the boat passed by.

Jackie's nine-day visit to India was a tremendous success. As she was leaving his country, Nehru said that she had helped improve the relations between India and the United States.[15]

Jackie's next stop was Pakistan. Drums pounded and cheering crowds showered Jackie with sweet-smelling flower petals on her arrival. Later, walking with President Ayub Khan through the famous Shalimar Gardens, Jackie said, "All my life, I have dreamed of coming to the Shalimar Gardens. It is even lovelier than I had imagined. I only wish my husband could be here."[16]

At the end of the India-Pakistan tour, Jackie and her sister flew back to London, Lee's home. Jackie stayed for three days, during which she had lunch with Queen Elizabeth II. Then Jackie returned to Washington, D.C. Several weeks later, she hosted one of her most distinguished evenings at the White House. All forty-nine Nobel Prize winners living in the Western Hemisphere were invited to the White House. Jackie persuaded Mary Hemingway, widow of the writer Ernest Hemingway, to allow some of his unpublished work to be read that night.

America's most-famous artists, writers, poets, and musicians were invited to a White House banquet that Jackie hosted for the French Minister of Culture André Malraux and his wife, Madeleine. André Malraux had escorted Jackie to museums during her visit to Paris. Now she personally guided him through the National Gallery in Washington, D.C. As a grand gesture of gratitude to the first lady, Malraux had arranged for the loan of Leonardo da Vinci's *Mona Lisa* to the United States. Thousands of Americans viewed this world-famous painting during the two weeks it was on display at the National Gallery in Washington, D.C.

In an extraordinary gathering of intelligence and talent, the Kennedys hosted a party for forty-nine Nobel Prize winners. Here, JFK speaks with writer Pearl S. Buck while Jackie converses with the poet Robert Frost.

Jackie's eye for detail and perfection knew no bounds. One day, for example, President Kennedy told Jackie that he saw a lot of crabgrass from his window. This motivated Jackie to find a solution to the weeds and crabgrass growing in the White House lawns. She asked a horticulturalist to design a rose garden for the White House. A fragrant garden of red,

At the National Gallery of Art, the mysterious Mona Lisa smiles down upon the Kennedys and French minister of culture André Malraux and his wife.

yellow, peach, and white roses was unveiled in June 1962. It became President Kennedy's favorite place to show dignitaries. The rose garden has since become a famous White House landmark.

During the summer of 1962, Jackie traveled with the president to Mexico. She wowed the crowds by speaking to them in Spanish. Once again Jackie proved to be an excellent goodwill ambassador. She appreciated people of all cultures and nationalities, not only abroad but at home as well.

President Kennedy was a strong supporter of the civil rights movement, African Americans' struggle for equality. Jackie agreed that it was a good idea for the president to send troops to maintain peace when the first African-American student enrolled at the University of Mississippi in September 1962. The first lady also changed the White House social conventions by including African Americans on every guest list she prepared.[17]

A few weeks later, Jackie canceled a state dinner on short notice. When the staff asked why, she explained that they would find out when the president gave a speech the next night.[18]

On October 22, 1962, President Kennedy spoke to the nation. He said that the Soviet Union had installed nuclear missiles on military bases in Cuba. These missiles were powerful enough to reach the United States. This incident, which became known as the Cuban Missile Crisis, caused panic throughout the world, especially in the United States. Fearing food shortages that would result from a nuclear attack, many Americans stocked up on canned goods and water. Some people quickly created bomb shelters—underground rooms of cement blocks and sandbags—to be used in case of attack.

The president offered his wife the chance to leave the White House and go to a safe place with their children. But Jackie showed great courage by choosing to stay in the White House while the president searched for a solution. By the end of the week, the Soviets removed the missiles. The thirteen-day crisis was over and the entire world was relieved.

The first lady did a great deal to make her husband's administration sparkle with culture and sophistication. But her most important priorities were Caroline and John Jr., her children. Jackie insisted that they learn good manners and respect for all people.[19]

Jackie hoped to give Caroline and John Jr. as normal a childhood as possible. She wanted their growing-up years to be happy and carefree. Jackie told her press secretary and President Kennedy's press secretary that she did not want the children's every move recorded by the press. "My press relations will be minimum information given, with maximum politeness," she said.[20]

The Secret Service agents were advised not to spoil the children with too much attention, and not to do things for them that they could do themselves. According to Jackie, "If you bungle raising your children, I don't think whatever else you do well matters very much."[21]

Caroline went to the nursery school Jackie had installed on the third floor of the White House. The other students were the children of the Kennedys' friends from before they came to the White House. Also included were the children of the president's cabinet members. The first lady personally invited the young son of the assistant press secretary, who was African American, to join the nursery school. This desegregated the school.[22]

The first lady took turns with the other parents helping the teacher in the classroom. When a dignitary visited the White House or a military band played for a special occasion, Jackie arranged for the children to watch.

The nursery school playground, besides being a home to many small animals, had swings and a trampoline. To protect the children's privacy, gardeners had planted a high wall of shrubs around the trampoline. But some afternoons, visitors to the White House might see the thirty-three-year-old first lady's head bobbing above the hedge as she bounced on the trampoline with her children.[23]

In December 1962, Jackie's press secretary announced that the Kennedys were expecting a third child. Americans were thrilled that the country's first family would have an addition.

Death in Dallas

In April 1963, Jackie announced that she was going to cancel her official activities. She planned to spend more time with Caroline and John Jr. while awaiting the birth of the baby due in September. But in August, while on vacation, Jackie felt a stab of sharp pain. She was rushed to the hospital, where emergency surgery was performed to deliver the baby. Patrick Bouvier Kennedy was born prematurely and suffered from lung problems. He died two days later.

Jackie and her husband cried together over their loss. The tragedy brought a new closeness to their marriage. Jackie told her husband, "There's just one thing I couldn't stand—if I ever lost you."[1] In private, Jackie stayed near the president, and he often held her in his arms.[2]

Throughout their marriage, the differences in their ages, priorities, and interests had caused tension between them. Jackie had been left alone for long periods of time while JFK was on the campaign trail. She was aware that her husband had not always been faithful to her during the course of their marriage. But they had dealt with these issues together. Jackie said, "It took a very long time for us to work everything out, but we did, and we were about to have a real life together."[3]

For their tenth wedding anniversary, Jackie gave her husband three books documenting their years at the White House. She also gave him a religious medal to replace the one he had put in baby Patrick's coffin. From the president, the first lady received a bracelet from Egypt. The Kennedys were leaving their marital troubles in the past. The young couple now often held hands and even embraced in public.[4]

But Jackie continued to mourn Patrick's death. President Kennedy worried that her continuing sadness was not good for their family or for the work the first couple had to do for the country.[5] Jackie spoke often with her sister, Lee. Through Lee, the Greek shipping billionaire Aristotle Onassis heard that Jackie was having a difficult time. Onassis suggested to Lee that Jackie come for a vacation cruise aboard his yacht, the *Christina*.

The president supported the idea, hoping it would help Jackie regain her health.[6] So Jackie, Lee, and some friends sailed with Onassis around the Greek islands. Jackie talked to her husband by phone every day from Greece. The sea air and rest proved helpful for the first lady.

Three months after Patrick's death, President Kennedy asked Jackie to travel with him to Texas. He said it would be important to his reelection campaign. Jackie, who generally avoided campaign stops, replied, "I'll campaign with you anywhere you want."[7] President Kennedy was delighted, but he warned her that he did not expect a friendly reception in the Lone Star state. The president said that many people in Texas were upset by his support of civil rights. Also, the Kennedy administration's willingness to compromise with the Soviets angered many others. Nasty jokes and hateful leaflets aimed at JFK circulated in Dallas before his arrival. Jackie agreed to go along. Her presence would help ease the tensions.[8]

Crowds cheered when the first couple landed in Texas. Bouquets of yellow roses, the symbol of Texas, were presented to Jackie in San Antonio and Houston. White House aides joked that more people came to see Jackie than the president.[9] On November 22, 1963, the third morning of the trip, the Kennedys arrived in Dallas.

It was a hot day, and the first couple was eager to start the motorcade. The president and first lady sat on the back seat of the presidential convertible limousine, the red roses between them. The governor of Texas, John Connally, and his wife, Nellie, rode in the front seat. Despite the blazing midday sun, thousands of enthusiastic people had turned out to see the Kennedys and cheer them along.

The first couple waved to the crowds lining the

Campaigning for reelection brought JFK and Jackie to Dallas on November 22, 1963.

streets of downtown Dallas. The motorcade traveled down Main Street and approached Dealey Plaza at 12:30 P.M. Just after they passed an old seven-story brick building called the Texas School Book Depository, Mrs. Connally turned to the president and said, "You can't say that Dallas isn't friendly to you today."[10]

JFK's response was cut off by a loud, shattering sound. Jackie saw her husband put his hands to his throat, a confused look on his face. In the front seat, Governor Connally grabbed his arm in pain and cried out, "No, No, No! They're going to kill us both."[11]

Another gunshot sounded. The bullet hit President Kennedy's head. Bleeding, he slumped into Jackie's lap. "My God, what are they doing?" she cried. "My God! They've killed my husband, Jack! Jack!"[12] Terrified and in shock, Jackie scrambled out of her seat and onto the trunk of the limousine. A Secret Service agent, Clint Hill, pushed Jackie back into the passenger seat. The tragic event was over in less than six seconds. The governor was wounded but survived the shooting.

The motorcade sped to Parkland Memorial Hospital. Jackie held her husband in her arms and cried, "He's dead—they've killed him. Oh Jack, oh Jack, I love you."[13] At the hospital, Jackie hugged JFK and would not let Clint Hill take him away. She said, "You know he's dead. Let me alone."[14]

Clint Hill took off his jacket and wrapped it around President Kennedy's wounded head. Jackie then let go of her husband's body. The back seat was covered with blood and red roses.

The first lady stayed with her husband in the emergency room. She dropped to her knees when a Catholic priest gave the last rites to the president.[15] Before the priest finished, Jackie took one of her rings and slipped it onto her husband's finger. This was an Irish custom meaning "together in life, together in death."[16] Then she stood up. At 2 P.M., an official broadcast announced that the forty-six-year-old president was dead, shot by an assassin. Later that same day, authorities arrested a man named Lee Harvey Oswald for the crime.

Jackie accompanied her husband's coffin aboard

the presidential plane, *Air Force One*. Onboard the aircraft, while still parked at Love Field in Dallas, Vice President Lyndon Baines Johnson took the oath making him the thirty-sixth president of the United States. His wife was at his side. Jackie, in her pink suit spotted with the president's blood, stood to his left. During the ceremony, she looked dazed and shocked.[17] After President Johnson took the oath, Mrs. Kennedy went to the rear of the plane. She spent the rest of the trip near her husband's coffin.

Once *Air Force One* took off, Jackie spoke with

As Jackie Kennedy stood at his side in shock, Vice President Johnson was sworn into office as president of the United States. Johnson's wife, Lady Bird, was at his other side.

President Kennedy's aides and comforted them. Several people suggested to Jackie that she change out of her blood-stained clothes. She refused, saying, "Let them see what they've done."[18]

During times of crisis, Jackie's true strength of character always came through. One of her strengths, her skill at organizing, was now put to work. Respect for history had guided her restoration of the White House. Now, that same high regard for history would serve as a guideline for the funeral arrangements, which she patterned after the funeral of former president Abraham Lincoln. While the plane carrying Kennedy's body was still in the air, Jackie coped with her own shock and grief and comforted members of JFK's staff.[19]

Attorney General Bobby Kennedy, Jackie's brother-in-law, met her when *Air Force One* landed in Washington, D.C. He told her a "communist" had been arrested for shooting the president. Jackie believed that her husband had devoted himself to the great causes of world peace and civil rights. His death was even more senseless, she said, because it happened at the hand of a "silly little Communist."[20]

Caroline and John Jr. had to be told about their father's death. Jackie could not bear to do it. She asked their nanny to tell them. Five-year-old Caroline understood the sad news, but John Jr., not quite three, asked when his father would come home.[21] Jackie arranged for the president's body to lie in state in the East Room, protected by the honor guard.

In keeping with her husband's commitment to civil rights, Jackie insisted the honor guard be integrated at all times.[22] The guards stood at attention, watching over the flag-draped casket. During a private visit, Jackie placed the religious medal she gave her husband for their tenth anniversary and letters from Caroline and John Jr. into his coffin.

The Kennedy family wanted the president to be buried at their family plot in Massachusetts. But Jackie felt he belonged to the American people and chose a burial site in Arlington National Cemetery.[23] The day before the funeral, the president's coffin was moved from the White House to the Capitol rotunda, where it lay in state. Thousands of people came to pay respect to the slain president.

On Monday, November 25, 1963—John Jr.'s third birthday—a riderless horse led the procession carrying the president's casket from the rotunda to St. Matthew's Church. A pair of black boots dangled backward from the horse's saddle to symbolize the slain president. Drums beat a slow steady rhythm. Mourners lined the streets. The thirty-four-year-old widow, along with Kennedy family members and heads of state from around the world, walked behind the horse-drawn wagon that carried the flag-draped coffin. As the procession passed, some people cried and others saluted.

At one point, Jackie leaned down and spoke to her son. He stepped forward and saluted his father's coffin. The sight of young John Jr. saluting remains an enduring image of President Kennedy's funeral.

The same priest who married the Kennedys conducted the graveside service at Arlington National

Cemetery. Jackie lit an eternal flame to burn at his grave day and night from that moment on.[24] She left the gravesite holding the arm of Bobby Kennedy and clutching the folded American flag that had covered her husband's casket.

Jackie never lost her composure as she walked to the church or at the funeral. Afterward, at a reception at the White House, she stood poised and gracious at the head of the receiving line. As people filed through to pay their respects, she thanked each one. In the past few days, she had lived through a great tragedy. Now, sad and exhausted, she soldiered on. This was her last time to be a hostess in the White House. And as with everything she did during those four sad days

in November, she set a powerful example of courage, grace, and dignity. Her strength helped the nation endure a terrible tragedy.

Jackie had always valued her privacy. She had worked hard to protect her children from news photographers and the glare of publicity. But the weekend of their father's funeral, she kept them at her side. In the rotunda, Caroline knelt by the flag-draped coffin. She

John Jr. was too young to understand that he would never see his father again.

kissed the flag and then slipped her small gloved hand under it to be closer to her slain father. Heartbreaking photographs of these two fatherless children and their sad, dignified mother brought the nation to tears. They are permanent images of American history from this tragic time.

Jackie wanted her children's lives to go on in a normal way. So that evening, as soon as her official duties were complete, Jackie gathered her immediate family and close friends for three-year-old John's birthday party. Later in the evening, after the children were in bed, and the crowds gone from the streets, Jackie and Bobby Kennedy went back to the gravesite. There she placed a spray of lilies of the valley on top of the fresh grave. Several weeks later, she arranged for Arabella and Patrick to be reburied near their father.

In the days following the funeral, Jackie put her own grieving aside to complete the last of her tasks as first lady. She personally thanked and said good-bye to all the White House staff. She wrote two special letters—a letter of gratitude to Secret Serviceman Clint Hill, who protected her husband, and a letter to the widow of a policeman who was killed by Lee Harvey Oswald before he was arrested.

Through the years, there has been speculation that more than one person was involved in the assassination of JFK. Jackie never commented publicly on this. One of President Johnson's first acts in office was to create a commission headed by Chief Justice Earl Warren to conduct an investigation into November 22, 1963. Jackie gave her testimony to the

Caroline and John Jr. were just young children when their father was assassinated.

Warren Commission. The commission concluded that Oswald had acted alone.

During JFK's thousand days in office, Jackie had helped him redesign the Presidential Medal of Freedom. As it turned out, the presentations of the medal were scheduled for the same day Jackie was to leave the White House. Robert Kennedy accepted the award on behalf of his slain brother. Jackie watched the ceremony, standing at a side door near the back of the room. No one saw her. She left before it ended.

Jackie and her children spent Thanksgiving at the Kennedy family compound in Hyannis Port. There, on a cold, stormy night, Jackie talked with journalist Theodore White about her husband and the events in Dallas. Both JFK and Jackie had a deep respect for history. "They shared the belief that history belongs to heroes; and heroes must not be forgotten," wrote White.[25]

Jackie told Theodore White that she was concerned about "bitter old men," who had published stories about the assassination.[26] Many of these stories were critical, sensationalized, or inaccurate. She wanted to set the record straight on JFK's presidency, his goals, and his accomplishments. She quoted President Kennedy's favorite line from the popular Broadway musical *Camelot:* "Don't let it be forgot, that once there was a spot, for one brief shining moment that was known as Camelot."[27]

Camelot was a mythological kingdom, a legendary land of high ideals. The wise, fair, and respected King Arthur ruled Camelot. Jackie wanted her husband to be remembered as a heroic man with honorable goals.

She compared JFK's noble vision for his country to King Arthur's high ideals for Camelot.[28]

Jackie had been described as a fairy-tale queen. Now she wanted JFK to be thought of as a modern-day King Arthur. She wanted his administration to be remembered as Camelot—a golden time in American history when the arts, culture, and civility were valued in the White house, a time when wise decisions were made. She said, "There'll never be another Camelot again. . . ."[29]

After Theodore White published the account of his conversation with Jackie, the American public readily accepted Jackie's linking of the Kennedy administration to Camelot.

Friends let Jackie and her children stay in their Georgetown home until she could find one of her own. When she bought a house several months later, it quickly became a tourist attraction. Daily, parades of buses stopped in front of her house. Strangers ran up to the children and tried to hug them. People tore the numbers off the front of the house. Upset by the unwanted attention, Jackie sold the Georgetown house.

Jackie realized she had to get away from a city with so many memories. It was important to her that Caroline and John Jr. remember their father's life, and not grow up trapped in the shadow of his death. Jackie moved with Caroline and John Jr. to New York, the city where she had grown up. There, together, they would begin a new life.

Moving On

As a child, Jackie had spent snowy winters in the city and warm summers by the sea. Now, twenty years later, Jackie and her children began spending winters in New York City and summers at a yellow and white barn-shaped house in New Jersey. During the difficult times in her childhood, Jackie had turned to horseback riding, books, and art for comfort. Once again, she found peace in these interests. Neighbors in New Jersey often saw Jackie jumping her horse over stone fences and racing between trees.

The move to New York was the third move in just over a year for the young family. To help her children feel at home, Jackie decorated their bedrooms in the same colors as in their White House rooms.[1]

The move from public to private life was not simple. Everything Jackie said or did was considered newsworthy. Widely admired for the way she conducted herself after the president's assassination, she had become the most famous woman in the world.[2]

Jackie knew that Caroline and John Jr. were going to be stalked by the press—constantly watched, written about, and photographed. She taught them to ignore what others wrote and said about them. Jackie worked hard to give her children feelings of self-worth based on their own interests and accomplishments.

Riding a horse at her New Jersey estate was a comforting distraction for Jackie.

Even though the small family had Secret Servicemen to guard them, the safety of her children became a major concern for Jackie.[3]

One day, Jackie and Caroline were walking home from church. A mentally ill woman came up to them and yelled insulting remarks about Jackie and JFK.[4] Jackie held Caroline close. A Secret Service agent pulled the woman away, and she was sent to a hospital. Jackie remained upset about the incident for many weeks.

Bobby Kennedy understood and shared Jackie's pain over the assassination. The former first lady and her brother-in-law spent many hours talking about the tragic event in Dallas. Their shared loss and grief became bonds that joined them.[5]

Jackie asked Bobby's advice on all important issues. He became a father figure to Caroline and John Jr. Because of his grief, Bobby was unsure about continuing his political career. Jackie encouraged him to stay in public service.[6] When he campaigned for a seat in the New York Senate, Jackie helped Bobby with his speeches, just as she had helped her husband.[7] Bobby won the race.

A few months after Jackie moved to New York City, President Johnson offered her an ambassadorship to France or Mexico. She turned him down. A future in politics did not interest her. Creating monuments to the memory of John F. Kennedy became the main outlet for Jackie's creativity.

She worked with an architect to design a permanent headstone and eternal flame at her husband's grave. Planning the John F. Kennedy

Memorial Library soon became Jackie's largest and most important project. The former first lady put the same artistic energy into creating the library as she did for the White House restoration.

Jackie organized a traveling exhibit to raise money to build the Kennedy Library. President Kennedy's treasured items, along with documents from his administration, were displayed in the show. In January 1964, Jackie appeared on television. She addressed the nation and thanked people for the thousands of letters that had been written to her after her husband died.

On the first anniversary of John F. Kennedy's assassination, in November 1964, many stores, government buildings, and homes across the country displayed pictures of President Kennedy. Newspapers and magazines featured articles on the slain president. Television and radio shows broadcast programs on the Kennedy years.

November 22 was a difficult day for Jackie. She spent the first anniversary of her husband's death sitting on a bench in Central Park, crying.[8] Her friends and family were concerned about her sad state of mind. When she spoke of JFK, she said, "I should have known that it was too much to dream that I might have grown old with him . . . I should have known that he was magic all along." Jackie had hoped her children would have two parents see them grow up. "Now he is a legend when he would have preferred to be a man," she said.[9]

After JFK's death, donations for his dream of a national cultural center began to pour in from all over the world. Congress decided to name the center after President Kennedy and dedicate it to his memory. On December 2, 1964, construction finally began for the John F. Kennedy Center for the Performing Arts.

In her emotional state, Jackie found it impossible to go back to the White House. When President Johnson renamed the White House Rose Garden the Jacqueline Kennedy Garden, Jackie sent her mother to accept the honor on her behalf. In May 1965, Queen Elizabeth II dedicated a memorial in Runnymede to President Kennedy. Jackie, Caroline, and John Jr. traveled to England for the event. Jackie cried during the ceremony.[10]

By this time, Jackie was looking with concern at the growing conflict in Vietnam. Early in her marriage, she had translated some French documents for JFK's speeches on the war in Indochina. By the time the Kennedys lived in the White House, the French had pulled out of the Southeast Asian conflict in bitter defeat. The French could no longer hold on to their colonies—Laos, Cambodia, and Vietnam. In addition, Vietnam was left divided. A Communist leader, Ho Chi Minh, controlled North Vietnam. Ngo Dinh Diem, a dictator and a devout Catholic, ruled South Vietnam.

In the early 1960s, President Kennedy had sent some military troops to South Vietnam to help the South Vietnamese resist being taken over by the Communists. By 1965, President Johnson had sent thousands of soldiers to fight in Vietnam. The conflict in Vietnam had become a war.

Though she never took a public stand on the Vietnam War, Jackie traveled on her own to Cambodia

Jackie and her children traveled to England when Queen Elizabeth II (left, in hat) held a ceremony to honor President Kennedy's memory. Next to the queen stands British Ambassador David Ormsby-Gore. On the right, Prince Philip holds John Jr.'s hand. In the back row, from left, are JFK's sister-in-law Pat Kennedy Lawford and his brothers Robert and Edward.

in November 1967. She hoped her presence would help ease tensions.[11] But the war in Vietnam continued. When Jackie returned home, she visited a veterans' hospital. Many of the soldiers were just eighteen or nineteen years old. Some were missing arms or legs; others were close to dying. Jackie spent a long time with each one, going from one patient to the next to show her concern for these men.[12]

Public pressure grew against President Johnson's support of the war in Vietnam. At this point in his presidency, Johnson was so unpopular that he decided not to seek reelection. With Johnson out of the race, Robert Kennedy announced his decision to run for president. Jackie attended several important functions on his behalf. Although she preferred to keep her children out of the spotlight, she allowed Caroline and John Jr. to be photographed with their devoted uncle.

While the Vietnam War dragged on overseas, Americans became increasingly divided over issues at home, such as the fight for civil rights. Violence erupted, and on April 4, 1968, thirty-nine-year-old Martin Luther King Jr. was assassinated in Memphis, Tennessee. Jackie had followed and supported Dr. King's leadership of the civil rights movement. His death affected her deeply. The night before King's funeral, Jackie visited the slain leader's family, then attended the burial ceremony in Atlanta the next day.

Soon after returning home from Georgia, Jackie introduced her mother and stepfather to her close friend Aristotle Onassis. Since her move to New York, the Greek billionaire had been a regular visitor. Their relationship grew from friendship to romance.

At first, the Auchinclosses thought Onassis was an unsuitable match for Jackie. He was twenty-three years older and of the Greek Orthodox faith. But he proved to be so gracious and kind that he won Jackie's mother over. Jackie's mother-in-law, Rose Kennedy, also liked Onassis and wanted Jackie to be happy.[13]

Bobby Kennedy did not care for Onassis. He told Jackie that he did not approve of some of Onassis's business practices.[14] In 1954, Onassis had been arrested by U.S. marshals and indicted by the Internal Revenue Service. Legal proceedings dragged on for two years. Finally the government had dropped criminal charges and Onassis paid $7 million to settle the civil suit against him.

Bobby Kennedy asked Jackie to keep her involvement with Onassis a secret until after the presidential election. Bobby was worried that her relationship might cost him votes. Jackie agreed to keep it private.[15] Early in the morning of June 5, 1968, Jackie received a phone call from Los Angeles. It was bad news.

Bobby Kennedy had won the California primary election for president. Then, just after Bobby's short victory speech, a gunman had shot him in the head as he walked though the kitchen of the Ambassador Hotel. Jackie immediately flew to Los Angeles.

Hundreds of people gathered outside the hospital, praying for Bobby Kennedy's recovery. He died the next afternoon with Jackie and two other family members at his bedside. The world reacted with shock at the assassination of a second Kennedy brother. Jackie comforted Bobby's wife, Ethel, and helped plan his funeral.

Now Jackie became even more frightened for the safety and well-being of her children. "I hate this country. I despise America, and I don't want my children to live here any more. If they are killing Kennedys, my kids are the number-one targets," Jackie said. "I want to get out of this country."[16]

By then, her relationship with Aristotle Onassis had become serious. They were discussing marriage. Jackie, age thirty-eight, had been a widow for close to five years. Caroline and John Jr. were ten and seven years old. Onassis had two adult children from his first marriage—a son, Alexander, and a daughter, Christina.

Jackie cared deeply for Onassis. He had a good sense of humor and extensive knowledge about Greek arts and culture. He was appealing for other reasons, too. His security team could protect Caroline and John Jr. Onassis owned the Greek island of Skorpios. He could provide a secure haven for Jackie and her children.

On October 20, 1968, a rainy night filled with the smell of jasmine and incense, thirty-nine-year-old Jacqueline Bouvier Kennedy married Aristotle Onassis. The candlelit ceremony was held in a Greek Orthodox church on Skorpios with only enough room for their immediate families.

American newspapers carried headlines such as, "America Has Lost a Saint" and "The Reaction Here Is

Many people were critical of Jackie's marriage to the Greek billionaire Aristotle Onassis.

Anger, Shock and Dismay."[17] For the past five years, Americans had thought of Jackie as a living symbol, a reminder to them of JFK and the ideals of Camelot. But in reality she was a single mother with two young children to protect.

The world's most admired woman now had worldwide disapproval. She also lacked the blessing of the Catholic Church. Many disappointed Americans did not understand or accept Jackie's choice to remarry.[18]

The marriage was an unusual one. Aristotle

Onassis continued to live on his yacht, the *Christina*, or in his apartment in Paris. Jackie spent a lot of time in Greece and learned to speak Greek. But because Caroline and John Jr. had been uprooted so many times in the previous few years, Jackie decided to continue making her home in New York City. Both children were enrolled in schools in Manhattan. Jackie wanted to be there with them.[19]

Caroline and John Jr. took friends to Skorpios during summer vacations. On school breaks, the family traveled throughout the Greek islands. They explored ruins and artifacts. Jackie wanted her children to learn about Greek history and the wisdom of the Greek poets and philosophers.[20]

Jackie also wanted her children to remember their father. In 1971, Jackie, Caroline, and John Jr. returned to the White House for the unveiling of the official portraits of President and Mrs. Kennedy. This was the first time they had been back in the home that they shared as a family.

On September 8, 1971, the John F. Kennedy Center for the Performing Arts opened as a "living memorial" to President Kennedy. For the gala opening, famed composer and conductor Leonard Bernstein wrote a new piece honoring JFK.

Although Jackie's marriage to Onassis did provide her with a private island and protection by his security force, the world was still fascinated by her. She was a constant target of paparazzi—the photographers who follow famous people in the hopes of getting a newsworthy picture or story. Wherever Jackie went, she was trailed by paparazzi. Many unauthorized pictures of her were published in newspapers and magazines.

For the first few years of their marriage, Jackie and Aristotle Onassis traveled between Greece, Paris, and New York. On January 22, 1973, tragedy struck. Onassis's son, Alexander, was badly injured in a plane crash. The couple was in New York at the time, and they rushed to be with Alexander. Jackie brought along a top neurosurgeon. But nothing could be done. Alexander's injuries were fatal.

Onassis never recovered from the death of his only son. There was nothing Jackie could do to make him happy. Soon he and Jackie started spending more time apart than together.[21]

Jackie was forty-six years old when Aristotle Onassis died on March 15, 1975. She issued a statement to the press explaining her gratitude to him for having brought light and happiness to her life during a sad time.[22] Later, Jackie inherited $20 million from Onassis's estate.

One day, over lunch, Jackie's friend Letitia Baldridge suggested that Jackie get a job. Jackie responded, "Who, me—*work*?"[23] But she grew to like the idea. She met with someone at Viking Press, who offered her a position as a literary editor. It was a perfect job for someone who loved books and reading. The forty-seven-year-old Jackie was about to begin a new chapter in her life.

Calm Waters

Like many other women, Jackie went back to work in midlife. On her first day at Viking, television news crews crowded the sidewalk outside the office building in New York City. Inside, Jackie's new coworkers did not know what to expect. They soon found that the former first lady worked hard and took her job seriously.

In 1977, Viking Press published a novel titled *Shall We Tell the President?* by British mystery writer Jeffrey Archer. The story describes an assassination attempt against the fictional president Teddy Kennedy. In real life, Edward "Teddy" Kennedy was a U.S. senator. He was JFK's youngest brother and Jackie's brother-in-law. Jackie had not read the book before it was published. When reviews came out, hinting that she was in some way responsible for the book's publication at Viking, she quit. That spring, Jackie accepted a job at Doubleday Publishers. She would work there for the next seventeen years.

At Doubleday, Jackie worked closely with authors, designers, artists, and marketing experts. In her small office, she made her own telephone calls and typed her own letters. Jackie edited biographies, collections of letters, photography books, and children's books.

The maternal instincts that Jackie had once reserved for Caroline and John Jr. now surfaced in the way she nurtured writers.[1] She gave her authors special attention and often made great efforts to find extra research materials for them. Jackie wanted the books she guided through publication to take readers on a fascinating journey.[2]

Jackie edited several high-profile celebrity biographies for Doubleday. But most of her work focused on fine-quality photography and art books. Jackie did all she could to help publicize her authors' books. The usually private Jackie Onassis made appearances at book parties for her authors.

Back in 1975, Jackie had selected a site at Dorchester's Columbia Point in Boston for another tribute to her husband: the Kennedy Library and Museum. She picked architect I.M. Pei to design the building. Jackie became involved in every aspect of the museum, from the design of the building to landscaping and, later, the exhibits.

Ten thousand people gathered in Boston on October 20, 1979, when the Kennedy Memorial

Library opened its doors. The entire Kennedy family attended the opening. President Jimmy Carter gave the dedication speech. For the rest of her life, the former first lady would attend Kennedy Library Foundation dinners and raise money for exhibits at the presidential library. Jackie cared deeply about the museum and John F. Kennedy's legacy.[3]

As first lady, Jackie had supported historic preservation. As a private citizen living in New York, she remained devoted to that cause on several fronts. She joined the committee to stop the destruction of Grand Central Terminal, a landmark building that was slated to be bulldozed. Her helpful support of the Municipal Arts Society led to her serving on its board of trustees. Jackie also joined the board of the Forty-second Street Development Corporation, whose goal

Jackie gathered with family and dignitaries at the opening of the John F. Kennedy Library in Boston. Pictured above are (1) Jackie, (2) Lady Bird Johnson, (3) Edward Kennedy, (4) Joan Kennedy, (5) Jimmy Carter, (6) Rosalynn Carter, and (7) Cardinal Medeiros of Boston.

was to improve the Times Square theater district, with its many restaurants and other tourist attractions. Money raised by the committee went toward making that area cleaner and safer.

Jackie's children were growing into adulthood. Over the years, she had worked hard to keep the memory of their father alive for them. Then, in the mid-1970s, a variety of books and articles had revealed new information about President Kennedy. Some of it reflected poorly on his presidency and his private life. The unfavorable view of an unfaithful husband had been kept from the public to protect President Kennedy's image.

Despite these negative facts, Jackie always wanted Caroline and John Jr. to remember their father with pride. She had arranged for friends and staff members from the Kennedy administration to spend time with the children so they could learn more about their father. These people told Caroline and John Jr. about JFK's good qualities and accomplishments.[4]

As time passed, Caroline and John Jr. both finished college and moved away from home. Caroline graduated from Radcliffe College of Harvard University in 1980 and from Columbia Law School in 1988. John Jr. graduated from Brown University in 1983 and received a law degree from New York University in 1989. Jackie had always been protective of her children and proud of their accomplishments. As adults, Caroline and John Jr. were devoted to and protective of Jackie.

The Kennedy Library remained important in Jackie's life. She encouraged her children to take center stage at library events, to participate in keeping their father's memory alive. In 1978 Jackie asked Caroline to commission a statue of JFK for Boston's Statehouse, where the Massachusetts legislature meets.

Jackie continued to balance her life with family, work, and travel. She had always been interested in many different subjects and ideas. Vacations had taken her through the southwest United States, Israel, and China. Now her work often led her to exotic places around the world, where she did in-depth research for the books she was editing.

When the Costume Institute of the Metropolitan Museum of Art in New York City featured a show of Russian clothing, she traveled to Russia to research the project, and she edited the catalog for the exhibit. In another project for the Metropolitan Museum of Art, the former first lady arranged for loans of historic court costumes from India and edited a book on Indian court life.

In 1981, Jackie bought land in Gay Head, on the southern tip of Martha's Vineyard, an island off Cape Cod. She built a nineteen-room house on 375 acres. She called it Red Gate Farm and stayed there each year from July to September. The house had many windows facing the sea, bringing the roar of the ocean into Red Gate's large rooms. Fireplaces warmed the house, which was filled with comfortable furniture. Jackie considered this home a base for her family.

Businessman Maurice Templesman was a frequent visitor at Red Gate Farm. Jackie had met him in the 1950s when he was an adviser on African

*The Kennedy Library was designed by architect I. M. Pei, known
for his distinctively shaped geometric buildings.*

affairs to President Kennedy. Although she had known him for many years, Jackie did not begin a romance with him until the early 1980s. The two enjoyed poetry, literature, history, and a love of the sea. They were constant companions and often spoke to each other in French.[5]

Templesman was different from Jackie's two husbands. He was not a billionaire or a public figure. A businessman, he was content to conduct their relationship outside the public eye. Jackie's friends said she had finally found peace and happiness.

Jackie never married Maurice Templesman. He had separated from his wife on friendly terms, but they were never divorced. Jackie became close to Templesman's three children and six grandchildren. Caroline and John Jr. also developed a warm relationship with Templesman. Jackie and her children called him "M.T."[6]

Doubleday Publishers promoted Jackie to senior editor in 1984. That same year, her thirty-nine-year-old half-sister, Janet, died of bone marrow cancer. Then Jackie's mother, Janet Auchincloss, developed Alzheimer's disease. In the past, Jackie and her mother often had a tense relationship. But during her mother's illness, Jackie visited her often. Janet Auchincloss died in 1989.

Jackie did not take public stands on political issues, with a few exceptions. When heads of state Nelson Mandela of South Africa and Mikial Gorbachev of Russia visited the United States, Jackie greeted them at the Kennedy Library. Her presence was her political statement.[7]

Nelson Mandela stirred up great controversy with his activism for civil rights in South Africa. By meeting with him in 1990, Jackie made it clear that she agreed with his ideals of racial equality.

Jackie's children were beginning to settle down. Her daughter, Caroline, married in 1986, when she was twenty-eight years old. She had met her husband, Edwin A. Schlossberg, at a dinner party in 1981. He has doctoral degrees in both science and literature and is thirteen years older than Caroline. He is also the founder of a company that designs educational and museum exhibits.

Jackie enjoyed a close relationship with her son-in-law. Over the next several years, Caroline and

Edwin had three children: Rose was born in 1988, Tatianna in 1990, and John in 1993. They called their grandmother "Grand Jackie," and Jackie looked forward to their weekly visits to her home.[8]

In her bedroom, Grand Jackie had a large wooden chest filled with colorful scarves, scraps of fabric, necklaces made of beads, and piles of rings with sparkling stones. When her grandchildren arrived, they dumped the chest onto the bedroom floor. Grand Jackie helped them make costumes from the fabrics and jewelry. Then she told her grandchildren stories while leading them through the apartment. Together they opened closets and peeked into darkened rooms looking for ghosts and make-believe creatures from Grand Jackie's stories. Jackie and her grandchildren sat on the living room floor and had a tea party after dress-up time.[9]

Jackie's apartment was on Fifth Avenue, across from the Metropolitan Museum of Art. When the weather was nice, she often took her grandchildren for walks in Central Park and bought them ice cream cones.

Jackie rarely talked about her time in the White House. The former first lady never got involved in any venture to make money from those days or in any scheme to take advantage of her fame. When books about her were published with information that was untrue, she ignored them. Jackie once told a friend that she did not read what was written about her.[10]

By the time she turned sixty, Jackie had made peace with her fame and the attention from the press. For privacy, she often wore large dark glasses. She covered her head with a scarf when she was out in public. By the late 1980s, people generally left her alone. She jogged around the Central Park reservoir almost every day, ate at diners, went shopping, and visited museums. Jackie took cabs instead of limousines. Once a cab driver heard her singing along with a song on the radio.

For many years, friends and relatives had asked Jackie to write her memoirs. But she had no interest in writing about herself. She told a friend that she would rather spend her time riding her horse or feeling the mist at Martha's Vineyard.[11]

When asked if she would be upset if someday historians used her letters and wrote about her, the former first lady answered, "I won't be here to mind."[12]

By 1986, twenty-five years had passed since Jackie had lived in the White House. Her sadness about the past had faded. Jackie proofread a book on the Kennedy administration written by American historian Arthur Schlesinger. She also gave interviews for her mother-in-law Rose Kennedy's autobiography. The former first lady contributed to a book on first ladies, allowing herself to be directly quoted. But privacy remained a priority. When Jackie gave an oral history to an author, she insisted that it not be made public until fifty years after John and Caroline had died.[13]

In June 1993, Jackie and Maurice Templesman took a trip to France. They visited the Provence region, where the Bouvier family had originated. Jackie turned sixty-four a month later. She was full of energy and very happy to have President Bill Clinton and his family visit her at Martha's Vineyard. President Clinton remembered visiting the White House as a teenager and shaking hands with his hero, President Kennedy. Clinton had been inspired to go into politics because of John F. Kennedy.[14]

In October 1993, Jackie made a public appearance at a rededication ceremony at the Kennedy Library. Caroline's husband had modernized the exhibit halls. In addition to items from the Kennedy presidency, displays showed the mood of the times in which her husband lived. Jackie wanted the museum to inspire young people. She wanted the library to be not just about politics, but also to show President Kennedy's values.

In December 1993, after spending Christmas with her family, Jackie and Maurice Templesman went on a vacation to the Caribbean. Jackie felt ill and returned early. In February 1994, Jackie's personal secretary made a public announcement: Jackie had non-Hodgkin's lymphoma, a type of cancer of the lymph system. Jackie stayed cheerful through rounds of chemotherapy and radiation. When she lost her hair as a result of chemotherapy, she wore turbans and joked about starting another fashion trend.[15]

Even as her condition worsened, Jackie kept up a heavy workload and spent time with family and close friends. Maurice Templesman moved his office into her apartment to help care for her.

On a warm, clear Sunday in May, Jackie looked frail when she walked in Central Park with Maurice Templesman, her daughter, and grandchildren.

Jackie went into the hospital the next day, May 16, 1994. When nothing more could be done for her, she went home to her apartment on May 18.

Hundreds of people stood on the sidewalk in front of her Fifth Avenue apartment building and prayed. Sixty-four-year-old Jacqueline Bouvier Kennedy Onassis died at 10:15 P.M. on May 19, 1994, with her children and Maurice Templesman by her bedside. At a private gathering held at Jackie's apartment the day before the funeral, her closed casket was covered with a colorful antique quilt from her bed.

The next morning, Caroline, John Jr., and Mr. Templesman spoke at the funeral service held in the church of St. Ignatius Loyola on Park Avenue in New York City. Jackie had been baptized and confirmed at this same church. Her son stressed how his mother's love of home, family, and friends, along with her sense of adventure, guided their choices for the readings at the funeral service.[16]

A chartered plane flew mourners to Washington, D.C., where Jackie was buried in Arlington Cemetary next to John F. Kennedy and their babies Arabella and Patrick. Her funeral was elegant in its simplicity. The eternal flame that Jackie lit for her husband now burns for her as well.

10

A Life Well Lived

In the weeks and months before her death, Jackie handwrote a list of personal gifts that she wanted to leave to friends. Most of her estate went to her children.

Over a lifetime of travels, Jackie had collected enough belongings to fill many storerooms. She knew that Caroline and John Jr. would not want to keep everything. Her will instructed them to sell the items they did not want.[1]

Caroline and John Jr. sorted through their mother's possessions. They donated many photographs, documents, and her wedding dress to the Kennedy Library. Then they arranged with a well-known auction house, Sotheby's, to sell the rest of Jackie's belongings.

Sotheby's published a catalog of the items and their estimated prices. On April 23, 1996, the first day of the auction, lines of shoppers gathered outside Sotheby's hours before it opened. Many people wanted to own a part of Jackie's life.

People bid large sums of money for even the smallest of Jackie's things. A silver-cased tape measure engraved with Jackie's initials, estimated at $500, sold for an astounding $48,875.[2] A small footstool with a torn, faded satin cover, worth $100, sold for

Jackie considered raising her children to be the most important job of her life. In 1999, a year after this photo was taken, John Jr. died in a plane accident. It was a terrible loss for a family that had already suffered so many tragedies.

$33,350.[3] By the end of four days of bidding, the sale of her items brought in $34 million, an amazing $29 million more than had been expected. Sotheby's donated $1 million to the Kennedy Library. The rest of the money went to her children.[4]

At the time of her death, Jackie had been famous for more than thirty years. Her husband had been elected president during an era of great hope and optimism in the United States. Americans were fascinated by Jackie's youth, intelligence, and elegant sense of style. Because she allowed very little information to be given out, the public always wanted to know more about her.

Jackie's restoration of the White House gave Americans a sense of pride in their past and the feeling that knowledge of American history was important. Jackie's support of the arts elevated Americans' awareness and pride in their own culture.

Jackie treated people of all races, cultures, and religions with respect. Her ability to speak foreign languages endeared her abroad as well as to Americans of all nationalities. When she traveled the world as first lady, she represented all that was good about the United States. With her belief in equal education for all children, she desegregated the White House preschool at a time when most schools in the country were segregated by race.

Jackie's sense of what was important never changed. She cared most about being a good mother to Caroline and John Jr. They grew up into successful, well-respected adults. She protected and nurtured the

Jackie's style, intelligence, and grace influenced so many parts of American life in the last part of the twentieth century.

memory of their father and helped them know about him and the good he did.

Once, at a dinner party, the host asked the guests what they thought was their greatest accomplishment. Jackie said that she considered herself sane even though she had lived through some very troublesome times.[5] The other guests were impressed that out of all she had done in her life, Jackie named that as her greatest feat. Fortunately for America, it was not her only feat.

During four sorrowful days in November 1963, when the nation was shocked and overwhelmed with sadness, Jackie's noble behavior held a grieving country together. Her respect for history guided her careful planning of the funeral proceedings. Through television, the Kennedy funeral was a historic media event. America and the world watched Jackie's calm, graceful conduct in the face of tragedy.

Throughout her life, no matter how difficult a situation was, Jackie put her own feelings aside and behaved with grace and dignity. She paved her own pathway. At her funeral, her brother-in-law, Senator Edward Kennedy of Massachusetts, said, "No one else looked like her, spoke like her, wrote like her, or was so original in the way she did things."[6]

When Jackie became first lady she symbolized the excitement, energy, and hopeful feeling of America in the early 1960s. Today her memory is revered and she remains an enduring symbol of courage, elegance, and style.

Chronology

1929—Jacqueline Lee Bouvier is born on July 28, 1929, in South Hampton, Long Island, New York.

1933—Her sister, Caroline Lee Bouvier, is born.

1940—Her parents, Janet and John V. Bouvier III, divorce on July 22, 1940.

1942—Janet Bouvier marries Hugh Auchincloss.

1944—Jackie enrolls at Miss Porter's, a Connecticut boarding school; joins the drama club; is an editor and cartoonist for the student paper.

1947—Enrolls at Vassar College.

1949—Spends her junior year studying in France.

1950—Transfers to George Washington University.

1951—Graduates with a bachelor's degree in French literature; meets John F. Kennedy.

1952—Becomes the "Inquiring Camera Girl" for the *Washington Times Herald*; begins to date John F. Kennedy.

1953—Marries John Fitzgerald Kennedy.

1957—Father, John Vernou Bouvier III, dies; daughter Caroline Bouvier Kennedy is born.

1960—JFK defeats Richard M. Nixon in presidential election; son John F. Kennedy Jr. is born.

1961—Becomes the third-youngest first lady of the United States; travels with President Kennedy to France and Austria.

1962—Tour of White House is televised.

1963—Newborn infant, Patrick, dies; President John F. Kennedy is assassinated on November 22, in Dallas, Texas.

1964—Jackie and her children move to New York City.

1968—Marries Aristotle Onassis on October 20.

1975—Aristotle Onassis dies in Paris.

1976—In September, begins her career in publishing as an assistant editor at Viking Press.

1978—Becomes an associate editor at Doubleday Publishers.

1979—John F. Kennedy Library and Museum opens in Boston.

1982—Is promoted to editor at Doubleday Publishers.

1986—Caroline Bouvier Kennedy marries Edwin Schlossberg.

1988—Jackie's first grandchild is born.

1994—Dies in her home in New York City on May 19; is buried at Arlington National Cemetery next to her first husband, John F. Kennedy Jr.

Chapter 1. Jackie Dazzles Paris

1. Carl Sferrazza Anthony, *As We Remember Her: Jacqueline Kennedy Onassis, In the Words of Her Family and Friends* (New York: HarperCollins, 1997), p. 150.

2. James Spada, *Jackie: Her Life in Pictures* (New York: St. Martin's Press, 2000), p.48.

3. Pamela Clarke Keogh, *Jackie Style* (New York: HarperCollins, 2001), p.112.

4. Ellen Ladowsky, *Jacqueline Kennedy Onassis* (New York: Random House, 1997), p. 96.

5. Ibid.

6. Arthur M. Schlesinger, *A Thousand Days: John F. Kennedy in the White House* (Boston: Houghton Mifflin Co., 1965), p. 356.

Chapter 2. Privileged Beginnings

1. John H. Davis, *Jacqueline Bouvier, An Intimate Memoir* (New York: John Wiley, & Sons, 1996), p. 8.

2. Stephen Birmingham, *Jacqueline Bouvier Kennedy Onassis* (New York: Grosset & Dunlap, 1969), p. 9.

3. Jan Pottker, *Janet and Jackie* (New York: St. Martin's Press, 2001), p. 67.

4. Donald Spoto, *Jacqueline Bouvier Kennedy Onassis: A Life* (New York: St. Martin's Press, 2000), p. 17.

5. John H. Davis, *Jacqueline Bouvier: An Intimate Memoir* (New York: John Wiley, & Sons, 1996), p. 21.

6. Bill Adler, ed., *The Uncommon Wisdom of Jacqueline Kennedy Onassis: A Portrait in Her Own Words* (New York: Citadel Press, 1994), p. 1.

7. Caroline Kennedy, *The Best Loved Poems of Jacqueline Kennedy Onassis* (New York, Hyperion, 2001), p. 71.

8. Ellen Ladowsky, *Jacqueline Kennedy Onassis* (New York: Random House, 1997), p. 8.

9. Spoto, p. 35.

10. Sarah Bradford, *America's Queen: The Life of Jacqueline Kennedy Onassis* (New York: Viking, 2000), p. 13.

11. Ibid., p. 14.

12. Adler, ed., p. 1.

13. Davis, p. 65.

14. Bradford, p. 10.

15. Spoto, p. 60.

16. Davis, p. 102.

Chapter 3. Adventure and Romance

1. Sarah Bradford, *America's Queen: The Life of Jacqueline Kennedy Onassis* (New York: Viking, 2000), p. 36.

2. John Davis, *Jacqueline Bouvier: An Intimate Memoir* (New York: John Wiley & Sons, Inc., 1996), p. 107.

3. Ibid., p. 109.

4. C. David Heyman, *A Woman Named Jackie* (New York: Carol Communications, 1988), p. 76.

5. Carl Sferrazza Anthony, *As We Remember Her: Jacqueline Kennedy Onassis, In the Words of Her Family and Friends* (New York: HarperCollins, 1997), p. 40.

6. Mary Van Rensselaer Thayer, *Jacqueline Bouvier Kennedy: The White House Years* (New York: Doubleday & Co., 1961), p. 79.

7. James Spada, *Jackie: Her Life in Pictures* (New York, St. Martin's Press, 2000). p. 12.

8. Bradford, p. 41.

9. Davis, p. 133.

10. Heyman, p. 83.

11. Anthony, p. 48.

12. Stephen Birmingham, *Jacqueline Bouvier Kennedy Onassis* (New York: Grossett & Dunlap, 1969), p. 61.

13. Davis, pp. 151–152.

14. Ibid., p. 151.

15. Ibid., p. 152.

16. Ibid., p. 153.

17. Spada, p. 12.

18. Heyman, p. 97.

19. Birmingham, p. 63.

20. Thayer, p. 88.

21. Ibid., p. 95.

22. Heyman, p. 115.

23. Bill Adler, ed., *The Uncommon Wisdom of Jacqueline Kennedy Onassis: A Portrait in Her Own Words* (New York: Citadel Press, 1994), p. 17.

24. Sarah Bradford, *America's Queen: The Life of Jacqueline Kennedy Onassis* (New York: Viking, 2000), p. 88.

25. Anthony, p. 86.

26. Heyman, p. 117.

Chapter 4. Political Partner

1. Carl Sferrazza Anthony, *As We Remember Her: Jacqueline Kennedy Onassis, In the Words of Her Family and Friends* (New York: HarperCollins, 1997), p. 77.

2. Sarah Bradford, *America's Queen: The Life of Jacqueline Kennedy Onassis* (New York: Viking Penguin, 2000), p. 13.

3. John H. Davis, *Jacqueline Bouvier: An Intimate Memoir* (New York: John Wiley & Sons, 1996), p. 193.

4. Donald Spoto, *Jacqueline Bouvier Kennedy Onassis: A Life* (New York: St. Martin's Press, 2000), p. 114.

5. Davis, p. 193.

6. James Spada, *Jackie: Her Life in Pictures* (New York: St. Martin's Press, 2000), p. 27.

7. Anthony, p. 93.

8. Ibid., p. 94.

9. John F. Kennedy, *Profiles in Courage* (New York: Harper, 1995), Introduction.

10. C. David Heyman, *A Woman Named Jackie* (New York: Carol Communications), 1988, p. 178.

11. Spoto, p. 136.

12. Ibid., p. 137.

13. Anthony, p. 101.

14. Heyman, p. 190.

15. Ibid., p. 198.

16. Bradford, p. 115.

17. Anthony, p. 110.

18. Spoto, p. 144.

19. Bill Adler, ed., *The Uncommon Wisdom of Jacqueline Kennedy Onassis: A Portrait in Her Own Words* (New York: Citadel Press, 1994), p. 42.

20. Anthony, p. 110.

21. Adler, ed., p. 65.

22. Heyman, p. 244.

Chapter 5. Life as First Lady

1. Caroline Kennedy, *Selections from the John F. Kennedy Library and Museum, Jacqueline Kennedy: The White House Years* (New York: Metropolitan Museum of Art, 2001), vii.

2. C. David Heyman, *A Woman Named Jackie* (New York: Carol Communications, 1988), p. 251.

3. Donald Spoto, *Jacqueline Bouvier Kennedy Onassis: A Life* (New York: St. Martin's Press, 2000), p. 166.

4. J.B. West, *Upstairs at the White House* (New York: Coward McCann & Geoghegan, Inc., 1973), p. 193.

5. Ibid., p. 197.

6. Mary Van Rensslaer Thayer, *Jacqueline Bouvier Kennedy: The White House Years* (New York: Doubleday & Co., 1961), p. 62.

7. Carl Sferrazza Anthony, *The Kennedy White House: Family Life and Pictures, 1961–1963* (New York: Simon & Schuster, 2001), p. 22.

8. Arthur M. Schlesinger Jr., *A Thousand Days: John F. Kennedy in the White House* (Boston: Houghton Mifflin, 1965), p. 8.

9. Bill Adler, ed., *The Uncommon Wisdom of Jacqueline Kennedy Onassis: A Portrait in Her Own Words* (New York: Citadel Press, 1994), p. 45.

10. Kathleen Craughwell-Varda, *Looking for Jackie* (New York: Fairstreet Productions and Welcome Enterprises, Hearst Books, 1999), p. 28.

11. Adler, ed., p. 51.

12. West, p. 236.

13. Sarah Bradford, *America's Queen: The Life of Jacqueline Kennedy Onassis,* (New York: Viking Penguin, 2000), p. 174.

14. Mary Barelli Gallager, *My Life with Jacqueline Kennedy* (New York: Paperback Library, 1969), p. 141.

15. Thayer, p. 114.

16. Schlesinger, p. 670.

17. Thayer, p. 114.

18. Adler, ed., p. 63.

19. Schlesinger, p. 367.

20. Ibid., p. 367.

21. Anthony, *The Kennedy White House,* p. 117.

22. James Spada, *Jackie: Her Life in Pictures* (New York: St. Martin's Press, 2000), p. 49.

23. Carl Sferrazza Anthony, *First Ladies, Volume II: The Saga of the Presidents' Wives and Their Power* (New York: Quill William Morrow, 1991), p. 71.

24. Anthony, *The Kennedy White House,* p. 145.

25. Heyman, pp. 344–345.

Chapter 6. Champion of the Arts

1. J.B. West, *Upstairs at the White House* (New York: Coward McCann & Geoghegan, Inc., 1973), p. 255.

2. Stephen Birmingham, *Jacqueline Bouvier Kennedy Onassis* (New York: Grosset & Dunlap, 1969), p. 109.

3. Donald Spoto, *Jacqueline Bouvier Kennedy Onassis: A Life* (New York: St. Martin's Press, 2000), p. 181.

4. Carl Sferrazza Anthony, *First Ladies, Volume II: The Saga of the Presidents' Wives and Their Power, 1961–1990* (New York: William Morrow, 1991), p. 37.

5. Spoto, p. 181.

6. Carl Sferrazza Anthony, *As We Remember Her: The Life of Jacqueline Kennedy Onassis, In the Words of Her Family and Friends* (New York: HarperCollins, 1997), p. 167.

7. Ibid.

8. Anthony, *First Ladies, Volume II*, p. 38.

9. Ibid., p. 40.

10. Ibid., p. 39.

11. Selections from the John F. Kennedy Library and Museum, *Jacqueline Kennedy: The White House Years* (New York: Metropolitan Museum of Art, 2001), p. 139.

12. Oleg Cassini, *A Thousand Days of Magic: Dressing Jacqueline Kennedy for the White House* (New York: Rizzoli, 1995), p. 121.

13. Editors of Life Magazine, *Remembering Jackie, A Life in Pictures* (New York: Warner Books, 1994), p. 72.

14. Ibid.

15. Jacqueline Duhême, *Mrs. Kennedy Goes Abroad* (New York: Workman Publishing Company, Inc., in Association with Callaway Editions, 1998), p. 50.

16. Ibid.

17. E. Fanny Granton, "The Lady in Black," *Ebony Magazine*, February 1964. p. 81.

18. West, p. 263.

19. Letitia Baldridge, *A Lady First* (New York: Viking, 2000), p. 180.

20. Bill Adler, ed., *The Uncommon Wisdom of Jacqueline Kennedy Onassis: A Portrait in Her Own Words* (New York: Citadel Press, 1994), p. 71.

21. Ibid., p. 95.

22. Carl Sferrazza Anthony, *First Ladies, Volume II: The Saga of the Presidents' Wives and Their Power, 1961–1990,* p. 90.

23. West, p. 217.

Chapter 7. Death in Dallas

1. William Manchester, *The Death of a President* (New York: Harper & Row, 1967), p. 8.

2. Carl Sferrazza Anthony, *As We Remember Her: The Life of Jacqueline Kennedy Onassis, In the Words of Her Family and Friends* (New York, HarperCollins, 1997), p. 193.

3. Donald Spoto, *Jacqueline Bouvier Kennedy Onassis: A Life* (New York: St. Martin's Press, 2000), p. 238.

4. Ibid., p. 216.

5. Anthony, p. 194.

6. Mary Barelli Gallager, *My Life with Jacqueline Kennedy* (New York: Coronet Communications, 1970), p. 295.

7. Manchester, p. 9.

8. Sarah Bradford, *America's Queen: The Life of Jacqueline Kennedy Onassis* (New York: Viking Penguin, 2000), p. 265.

9. Ibid.

10. United Press International, compiled by Four Days, "The Historical Record of the Death of President Kennedy," *United Press International and American Heritage Magazine,* 1964, p. 14.

11. Manchester, p. 157.

12. Ibid., p. 160.

13. Ibid., p. 163.

14. Ibid., p. 171.

15. Ibid., p. 216.

16. Wes Gallagher, supervising ed., Keith Fuller, *The Torch Is Passed . . . , The Associated Press Story of the Death of a President,* U.S.A.: Western Printing & Lithographing Co. 1961, p. 15.

17. Manchester, p. 324.

18. Ibid., p. 348.
19. Ibid., pp. 350–351.
20. Ibid., p. 407.
21. Ibid., p. 465.
22. E. Fannie Granton, "The Lady in Black," *Ebony Magazine*, February 1964, p. 81.
23. Anthony, *The Kennedy White House: Family Life and Pictures, 1961–1963* (New York: Simon & Schuster, 2001), p. 273.
24. Manchester, p. 550.
25. Theodore White, *In Search of History* (New York: Harper & Row, 1978), p. 523.
26. Ibid.
27. Ibid.
28. Ibid., p. 525.
29. Ibid., p. 523.

Chapter 8. Moving On

1. C. David Heyman, *A Woman Named Jackie* (New York: Carol Communications, 1988), p. 426.
2. Stephen Birmingham, *Jacqueline Bouvier Kennedy Onassis* (New York: Grosset & Dunlap, 1969). p. 131.
3. Sarah Bradford, *American's Queen: The Life of Jacqueline Kennedy Onassis* (New York: Viking Penguin, 2000), pp. 322–323.
4. Heyman, p. 443.
5. Bradford, p. 303.
6. Heyman, p. 428.
7. Jay Mulvaney, *Diana & Jackie: Maidens, Mothers, Myths* (New York: St. Martin's, 2002), p. 243.
8. Heyman, p. 437.
9. Carl Sferrazza Anthony, *As We Remember Her: The Life of Jacqueline Kennedy Onassis, In the Words of Her Family and Friends* (New York, HarperCollins, 1997), pp. 220–221.

10. Christopher Anderson, *Jackie After Jack, Portrait of the Lady* (New York: William Morrow and Company, Inc., 1998), p. 130.

11. Anthony, p. 232.

12. Ibid., p. 234.

13. Ibid., pp. 240–241.

14. Anderson, p. 164.

15. Anderson, pp. 172–173.

16. Heyman, p. 486.

17. Ibid., p. 497.

18. Ibid.

19. Spoto, p. 275.

20. Caroline Kennedy, ed., *The Best Loved Poems of Jacqueline Kennedy Onassis* (New York: Hyperion, 2001), p. 71.

21. Spoto, pp. 258–259.

22. Birmingham, p. 198.

23. Ibid., p. 206.

Chapter 9. Calm Waters

1. Carl Sferrazza Anthony, *As We Remember Her: The Life of Jacqueline Kennedy Onassis, In the Words of Her Family and Friends* (New York: HarperCollins, 1997), p. 321.

2. Lester David, *Jacqueline Kennedy Onassis: A Portrait of Her Private Years* (New York: Birch Lane Press, 1994), p. 173.

3. Christopher Anderson, *Jackie After Jack, Portrait of the Lady* (New York: William Morrow and Company, Inc., 1998), p. 341.

4. Ibid., p. 267.

5. Sarah Bradford, *American's Queen: The Life of Jacqueline Kennedy Onassis* (New York: Viking Penguin, 2000), p. 418.

6. Anthony, p. 302.

7. Donald Spoto, *Jacqueline Bouvier Kennedy Onassis: A Life* (New York: St. Martin's Press, 2000), pp. 252–253.

8. James Spada, *Jackie: Her Life in Pictures* (New York: St. Martin's Press, 2000), p. 161.

9. Anderson, pp. 407–408.

10. Anthony, p. 333.

11. Bill Adler, ed., *The Uncommon Wisdom of Jacqueline Kennedy Onassis: A Portrait in Her Own Words* (New York: Citadel Press, 1994), p. 150.

12. Adler, ed., p. 145.

13. Anthony, p. 336.

14. Anderson, p. 411.

15. Ibid., p. 419.

16. Jay Mulvaney, *Diana & Jackie, Maidens, Mothers, Myths* (New York: St. Martin's Press, 2002), p. 290.

Chapter 10. A Life Well Lived

1. Bill Adler, *The Last Will and Testament of Jacqueline Kennedy Onassis* (New York: Carroll & Graf Publishers, Inc. 1997), Section E, Paragraph 1, p. 2.

2. Sotheby's catalog, *The Estate of Jacqueline Kennedy Onassis*, April 23–26 (New York: Sotheby's, 1996).

3. Sotheby's, p. 10.

4. Adler, ed., Section E, Paragraph 1.

5. C. David Heyman, *A Woman Named Jackie* (New York: Carol Communications, 1988), p. 579.

6. Lester David, *Jacqueline Kennedy Onassis: A Portrait of Her Private Years* (New York: Birch Lane Press, 1994), p. 221.

Further Reading

Adler, Bill, ed. *The Uncommon Wisdom of Jacqueline Kennedy Onassis: A Portrait in Her Own Words.* New York: Carol Publishing Group, 1994.

Anthony, Carl Sferrazza. *The Kennedy White House: Family Life and Pictures, 1961–1963.* New York: Simon and Schuster, 2001.

Cassini, Oleg. *A Thousand Days of Magic.* New York: Rizzoli International Publications, Inc., 1995.

Davis, John H. *Jacqueline Bouvier: An Intimate Memoir.* New York: John Wiley & Sons, Inc., 1996.

Flaherty, Tina Santi. *What Jackie Taught Us: Lessons from the Remarkable Life of Jacqueline Kennedy Onassis.* New York: The Berkeley Publishing Group, 2004.

Gormley, Beatrice. *Jacqueline Kennedy Onassis: A Friend of the Arts.* New York: Aladdin, 2002.

Editors of Life Magazine. *Remembering Jackie: A Life in Pictures.* New York: Warner Books, 1994.

Arlington National Cemetery—Jacqueline Kennedy Onassis

<http://www.arlingtoncemetery.net/jbk.htm>

This site contains two articles written after Jacqueline Kennedy Onassis's death. Both articles include biographical information with quotes from family, friends, authors, and political figures.

John F. Kennedy Presidential Library & Museum— Jacqueline Bouvier Kennedy

<http://www.jfklibrary.org>

This site has an easy-to-read biography. Click on Biographies & Profiles under Historical Resources. Then click on Jacqueline Bouvier Kennedy under Biographies.

John F. Kennedy Library and Museum—Jacqueline Bouvier Kennedy, the White House, and Preservation

<http://www.cs.umb.edu/~rwhealan/jfk/jbkwh. htm>

This site spotlights Jacqueline Bouvier Kennedy's role in restoring the White House and includes illustrations of restored rooms.

Index

Page numbers for photographs are in **boldface** type.

92 Onassis
Agins, Donna Brown.
Jacqueline Kennedy Onassis